# Christmas

## 1990

*Everywhere, everywhere Christmas—*
*Throughout the land,*
*Within the heart,*
*Beside the hearth.*

**Meredith® Press**
New York, New York

**FOR MEREDITH® PRESS**

Director: Elizabeth P. Rice
Editorial Project Manager: Maryanne Bannon
Contributing Editors: Lori Labriola (Recipes)
Barbara Machtiger (Text)
Cyndi Marsico (Crafts)
Staff Writer: Maryanne Bannon
Production (Film and Separations): Bill Rose
Design: Remo Cosentino/Bookgraphics
Cover Photograph: Nancy Palubniak
Prop Stylist: Diane Wagner
Assistant: Ruth Weadock

May there come to you at this Holiday Time
An abundance of the precious things of Life:
Health, Happiness and Enduring Friendships.

*Abraham Lincoln*

# TABLE OF CONTENTS

# CHRISTMAS WITHIN THE HEART

# CHRISTMAS BESIDE THE HEARTH

*Everywhere,*
*Everywhere*
*Christmas*
*Tonight*

Christmas in lands of the fir tree and pine,
Christmas in lands of the palm tree and vine;
Christmas where snow peaks stand solemn and white,
Christmas where cornfields lie sunny and bright;
Everywhere, everywhere Christmas tonight!

Each year over 350,000 spectators turn out to enjoy Denver, Colorado's Parade of Lights.

Luminaria cast a soft glow over the mission of San Felipe de Neri in Albuquerque, New Mexico.

The Salvation Army joins Rockefeller Center's sculpted angels in heralding the season in New York City.

So the stars of the midnight which compass us round,
Shall see a strange glory and hear a sweet sound,
And cry, "Look! the earth is aflame with delight.
Oh sons of the morning rejoice at the sight."
Everywhere, everywhere Christmas tonight!

*Phillips Brooks*

The stark beauty of the Saguaro cactus is limned against the desert
sky in Phoenix, Arizona.

Carolers sail the *Spirit of Seattle* bringing the music of the season
to residents of Elliot Bay and Lake Washington.

9

# *The Reverend Schwan's Christmas Tree*

Christmas in America was not always celebrated with the national outpouring of joy and goodwill that it is today. In 1851 the influence of the Puritans, who had outlawed Christmas celebrations as pagan abominations, still permeated the country's social mores. Only ten states recognized Christmas as a legal holiday, and in some regions, like New England, even private celebrations were few. Christmas trees were rare and displayed only in the home, usually those of German immigrants, who brought their Old World tradition to our shores.

The Reverend Heinrich Christian Schwan arrived in Cleveland in 1851 as the new pastor of the Zion Lutheran Church. The Reverend had grown up with the delightful custom of the Christmas tree and wished to share this happy symbol of Christ's birth with his new congregation. The church tree was modestly decorated with colored ribbons, paper chains, tinsel, cookies, nuts, and small toys. Lighted candles graced the green boughs and a cherished silver star, brought from Germany, topped the tree.

A public uproar ensued, despite the obvious delight of the children and some of the congregation. *The Cleveland Leader* declared the tree "a nonsensical, asinine, moronic absurdity, besides being silly." The good pastor was villified as an idolatrous pagan "groveling before a bush." But the tree remained.

Hoping to retain the lovely custom, but not wishing to offend his congregation, Reverend Schwan quietly campaigned for the next year's Christmas tree. By the end of 1852, *The Plain Dealer*, a respected local newspaper, was extolling the Christian symbolism of the Christmas tree. In the Zion Lutheran Church, a Christmas tree was once again displayed for all to see and admire.

The site of that first public Christmas tree was declared a national historical location in 1976. So everytime you enjoy the beauty and wonder of a Christmas tree, remember the courage and wisdom of a modest Lutheran pastor in Cleveland in 1851.

# *Go Tell It on the Mountain*

Go tell it on the mountain,
Over the hills and everywhere,
Go tell it on the mountain,
That Jesus Christ is born.

When I was a sinner,
I prayed both night and day;
I asked the Lord to help me,
And He showed me the way.

When I was a seeker,
I sought both night and day;
I asked the Lord to help me,
And He taught me how to pray.

Down in a lowly manger
The humble Christ was born,
And God sent out salvation
That blessed Christmas morn.

*American Black Spiritual*

# America's Bright Idea

Y ou've carefully hung every cherished ornament and draped the silver icicles just so on the fresh green boughs. The decorating of this year's Christmas tree is finished, but the effect is not complete—not yet. The room lights are dimmed and then—magic! The icicles are now glimmering strands of the rainbow and the ornaments sparkle like so many brilliant jewels. The tree glows with the enchantment of light and color.

We of the late twentieth century can hardly appreciate the wonder and awe electric lighting was greeted with by our great-grandparents and their offspring. Yet during the Christmas season, even we are compelled to admire and exclaim over the

magical effect of garlands of gleaming lights transforming our homes and towns into shimmering wonderlands.

When Thomas Edison invented the first successful light bulb in October, 1879, it was for utilitarian purposes. But the decorative possibilities of electric lights soon became evident. In 1882 the vice-president of Edison's electric company, Edward H. Johnson, festooned his Christmas tree with 80 tiny red, white, and blue hand-blown and hand-wired lamps, as light bulbs were then called. A new tradition, a uniquely American contribution to the Christmas celebration, was born.

Costing more than the modern equivalent of $1,000, family

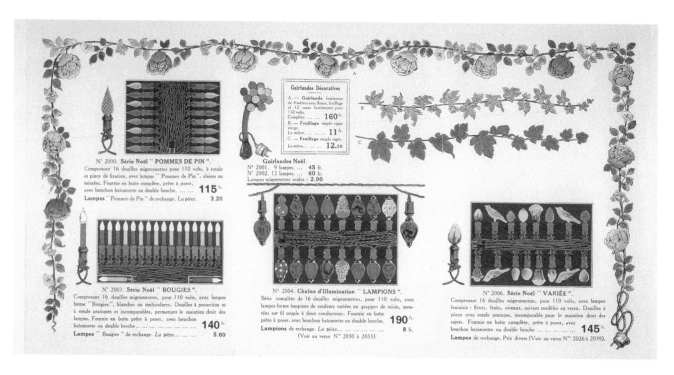

Christmas trees decorated with electric lights were then the exclusive delight of the very rich. It wasn't until 1903, when the Ever Ready Company of New York mass-produced 28-socket strings of lights, called "festoons" or "outfits," that middle-class families, by diligent penny-pinching, might hope to similarly adorn their trees.

Commercial production of electric light outfits made development of decorative bulbs economically feasible for manufacturers. The first Christmas bulbs were miniaturized versions of the common household bulb dipped in paint. In 1909 exquisite hand-made and hand-painted figurative miniature bulbs were imported from Austria. Trees could be trimmed with softly glowing fruits, flowers, birds, animals, fairy-tale characters, even Santa. The now standard cone-shaped bulb, developed by General Electric during the 1920s, was then considered a novelty.

Unfortunately, many families of the early twentieth century were unable to enjoy the wonder and delight of electric Christmas tree lights. Not all homes were hooked up to electric lines and for many more, the cost of a lighting outfit was still prohibitive. So that all its citizens could enjoy the wonder and beauty of an electric tree, Pasadena, California, lighted the first communal Christmas tree in 1909. Very quickly, public-spirited individuals and civic

organizations were sponsoring Christmas tree lighting ceremonies in communities across the nation. In New York City, a crowd of 10,000 people gathered in Madison Square Park for the lighting of the city's first tree in 1912, and as the 3,500 lights burst into glowing color, thrilled spectators became spontaneous carolers of Christmas songs and hymns.

Public lighting displays became a source of civic pride and community spirit. As the use of electric lighting spread, cities and towns of all sizes began staging contests for the best lighting designs. In 1922, 300 participants entered Denver's first competition. Categories and prizes were established for various business and residential installations. By 1925 over 1,600 displays of all types were recorded. Denver

declared itself the Queen City of Outdoor Christmas Lighting. Competition was fierce, however, and cities and towns from rustic Caspar, Wyoming, to glamorous Beverly Hills, California, challenged Denver's claim. Silent film star Mary Pickford headed a committee that organized the simultaneous lighting of over 800 live Christmas trees across the Beverly hills.

Although the technical and economic reasons for communal Christmas trees have long disappeared, the popular novelty of the early century is now a cherished custom. It is only fitting that as we celebrate the birth of Christ, Light of the World, that the spirit of love and joy go beyond the narrow confines of our homes to the greater community of town and country.

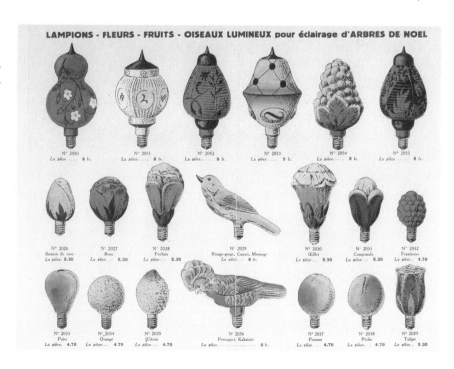

# The Three Kings

HENRY WADSWORTH LONGFELLOW

They thought the Wise Men were men insane,
As they spurred their horses across the plain,
Like riders in haste, and who cannot wait.

And when they came to Jerusalem,
Herod the Great, who had heard this thing,
Sent for the Wise Men and questioned them;
And said, "Go down unto Bethlehem,
And bring me tidings of this new King."

Three Kings came riding from far away,
Melchior and Gaspar and Baltasar;
Three Wise Men out of the East were they,
And they travelled by night and they slept by day,
For their guide was a beautiful, wonderful star.

The star was so beautiful, large, and clear,
That all the other stars of the sky
Became a white mist in the atmosphere,
And by this they knew that the coming was near
Of the Prince foretold in the prophecy.

Three caskets they bore on their saddlebows,
Three caskets of gold with golden keys;
Their robes were of crimson silk with rows
Of bells and pomegranates and furbelows,
Their turbans like blossoming almond-trees.

And so the Three Kings rode into the West,
Through the dusk of night, over hill and dell,
And sometimes they nodded with beard on breast,
And sometimes talked, as they paused to rest,
With the people they met at some wayside well.
"Of the Child that is born," said Baltasar,
"Good people, I pray you, tell us the news;
For we in the East have seen His star,
And have ridden fast, and have ridden far,
To find and worship the King of the Jews."

And the people answered, "You ask in vain;
We know of no king but Herod the Great!"

So they rode away; and the star stood still,
The only one in the gray of morn;
Yes, it stopped,—it stood still of its own free will,
Right over Bethlehem on the hill,
The city of David, where Christ was born.

And the Three Kings rode through the gate
        and the guard,
Through the silent street, till their horses turned
And neighed as they entered the great inn-yard;
But the windows were closed, and the doors
        were barred,
And only a light in the stable burned.

And cradled there in the scented hay,
In the air made sweet by the breath of kine,

The little Child in the manger lay,
The Child, that would be King one day
Of a kingdom not human but divine.

His mother Mary of Nazareth
Sat watching beside His place of rest,
Watching the even flow of His breath,
For the joy of life and the terror of death
Were mingled together in her breast.

They laid their offerings at His feet:
The gold was their tribute to a King,
The frankincense, with its odor sweet,

Was for the Priest, the Paraclete,
The myrrh for the body's burying.

And the mother wondered and bowed her head,
And sat as still as a statue of stone;
Her heart was troubled yet comforted,
Remembering what the Angel had said
Of an endless reign and of David's throne.

Then the Kings rode out of the city gate,
With a clatter of hoofs in proud array;
But they went not back to Herod the Great,
For they knew his malice and feared his hate,
And returned to their homes by another way.

# Santa: The Living Legend

When I was still wearing flannel pajamas with padded feet, my younger brother and I conspired to catch a glimpse of Santa Claus. With absolute certainty, we knew that if we could stay awake until midnight, we would hear Santa's sleigh on the roof. We huddled, wrapped in our blankets, around the dim night-light that prevented spills down the attic stairs. Our biggest worry was the weather. It was Christmas Eve and there wasn't a snowflake in sight. Did Santa need snow to make his yearly visit? Fearing discovery, our debate was whispered but intense. And though we nodded off well before Santa's appointed hour, the next morning bore witness to the truth. Santa Claus was as real as you or I. It mattered not at all that this magical benefactor was a relative newcomer to the Christmas celebration—a uniquely American character with a family tree deeply rooted in mythology and legend.

Some scholars trace Santa's ancestral beginnings a thousand years before St. Nicholas, to the white-bearded Greek god Kronos, father of the gods, and his Roman counterpart, Saturn. Romans celebrated the seven-

day festival of Saturnalia, which began on December 17, with gift-giving and feasting. It commemorated Saturn's golden age, when peace reigned, earth gave of her bounty, rivers flowed with wine and fountains with milk and honey, men were free and all were good.

Yet, Saturn had a malevolent side. According to myth, in order to ensure his dominion was not usurped by his progeny, he ate his children. Perhaps because they are timeless allegories about human nature, myths evolve rather than disappear and often cross cultural barriers: Long after the occupying Roman legions were gone, vestiges of this paternal violence were apparent in the local legends of fifteenth-century Germany. The early medieval concept of St. Nicholas included both reward for the deserving and rebuke for the wicked. By then, however, St. Nicholas had become all-good but had acquired a harsh, evil twin to mete out punishment. German parents admonished their children that not only would St. Nicholas overlook bad boys and girls, but that the legendary *Kindleinfresser*, or children eater, hearing of their wickedness, would snatch them away, stuffing the disobedient into his bag and carrying them off, never to be seen again.

Happily, our Santa Claus descends from the kinder aspect of St. Nicholas, a legendary bishop of early Christianity renowned for his generosity and

goodness. Whether Nicholas was, in fact, a real person or the creation of man's imagination, no one really knows, as there is no historical evidence of his life.

Roman accounts of Nicholas have him as the son of wealthy Greek Christians, born in A.D. 270 in the Mediterranean city of Lycia, now a part of Turkey. His holiness was evident even as a child, and when orphaned at age nine, he entered a Lycian seminary.

Years later, as bishop of Myra, he was already the subject of legend. An often-told tale is that of the three beautiful, but poor, sisters. Without money for dowries they could not marry, so the eldest sister sought to sell herself into slavery that her sisters might find husbands. Hearing of this unselfish act, Nicholas stole by the sisters' home one night, throwing three bags of gold, one for each girl, through the open win-

dow. Some versions of the story have the bags being thrown down the chimney and one landing in a stocking hanging to dry by the fire!

Nicholas lived out his life as bishop of Myra, his generosity a legend in his own time. His death is given as December 6, A.D. 340.

Although no written accounts of Nicholas existed until the ninth century, as Christianity became the religion of the people, Nicholas's fame grew. During the Middle Ages, his popularity rivaled that of Mary, the mother of Jesus. In England there were more than twice as many churches dedicated to Nicholas as there were to St. George, England's patron saint. Russia, Greece, and Sicily declared Nicholas their patron, as did sailors, lawyers, travelers, students, fishermen, and many others. But he was best known as the special saint and protector of little children.

In the thirteenth century, French nuns began the custom of giving gifts to the poor on the eve of his saint's day, December 6. The practice enjoyed quick popularity and as St. Nicholas was the particular patron of children, it soon became their special festival. This tradition continues throughout Europe today, most notably in Holland.

The Protestant Reformation eliminated all saints, even Nicholas, so Martin Luther created a new figure in the Christmas roster. The *Christkindlein*, or Christchild, a holy youth, wandered alone examining the behavior of children and adults alike. Once assured of their goodness, he distributed gifts to the deserving. Other locales substituted secular figures to take Nicholas's place. For example, in England there was Father Christmas, in France *Père Noël*, and in Germany the *Wiehnachtsmann*. However, St. Nicholas did not disappear totally. Although outlawed in the Netherlands, St. Nicholas and his traditions continued to be cherished in Dutch homes, however secretly. And those areas that remained Catholic still revered him as a saint and kept the old customs alive.

These many variations of the gift-bearer landed on our shores with our ancestors, and through that uniquely American phenomenon, the melting pot, gradually evolved into the magical, appealing gentleman we've come to know as Santa Claus. Our Santa is the end product of an ancient Christian legend brought to the New World by the Dutch, rediscovered and retold by a Scotsman, whose tale inspired a descendant of early English settlers, whose literary creation was brought to life by a German artist.

In 1809 Washington Irving, a New Yorker of Scottish descent, delighted Americans—city dwellers as well as frontiersmen—with "A History of New York from the Beginning of the World to the End of the Dutch Dynasty by Diedrich Knickerbocker." In it he vividly recounts a visit from St. Nicholas, who arrives driving his wagon over the tree tops of New Amsterdam

to deliver his yearly bounty. Irving's wonderfully fertile imagination provided tongue-in-cheek accounts of the ship *Goede Vrouw*, with its figurehead of St. Nicholas; St. Nicholas Day celebrations in New Amsterdam; and the colony's first church dedicated to the saint. In fact, Nicholas was almost unknown in the New World until Irving successfully reinvented history.

Legend was stronger than fact, however, and in 1822 Clement Moore created "A Visit from St. Nicholas." Little

did he realize that the 56-line poem written to amuse his children would take on mythic proportions, to be considered by many the definitive account of Santa Claus, to be consulted as one would a revered authority.

Moore was from an old, wealthy New York family of English ancestry; a professor of Greek literature and Biblical languages. Using a neighbor as his model, Moore transformed the ascetic bishop of Myra into a plump, jolly elf.

20

Through an informal network of friends and relatives, "A Visit from St. Nicholas" first reached the public in a local newspaper in Troy, New York. The popularity and influence of this poem was truly astounding. Within a generation, Moore's happy elf had become America's interpretation of the St. Nicholas legend.

Although Moore's poem referred to St. Nicholas, like so many new Americans, he too would undergo a name change. *Sint Nikolass* had come to these shores with the Dutch, who contracted his name to *Sinterklass* in the days of New Amsterdam. As the English transformed New Amsterdam to New York, *Sinterklass* was Anglicized to Santa Claus. Sometime during the mid-nineteenth century Americans began to commonly refer to St. Nicholas as Santa Claus.

Thomas Nast, a German immigrant and an accomplished illustrator, completed St. Nicholas's transformation from the thin bishop with cape and mitre to the rotund, jovial figure of Santa Claus. Moore had described Santa Claus, but it was Nast who gave him flesh and blood. From 1863 until 1886 Nast created his special Christmas illustrations for *Harper's Weekly* .

It is these pen-and-ink drawings that define Santa's appearance even to this day.

The matter of Santa's costume was the stuff of raging debates in the latter half of the nineteenth century. Moore had described St. Nick as fur-clad, but style and color choice was left to individual preferences. Sometimes Santa wore long fur coats, often green, occasionally blue. Buckskin trousers and boots was not an uncommon outfit for Santa. In 1866 Nast illustrated a children's book, one of the first to be printed in color, *Santa Claus and His Works*, by George P. Walker. Nast pictured Santa wearing a brownish-red fur suit trimmed with white fur. But it was the advent of the department store Santa that gradually standarized Santa's costume. In 1890 the round, white-bearded owner of The Boston Store in Brockton, Massachusetts, decided to give the children of the town a unique treat. James Edgar ordered a custom-made suit and played Santa Claus for his youngest customers. News of this Santa spread like wildfire. Families travelled from as far away as Providence, Rhode Island, to visit this real, breathing Santa. Even in distant New York, children knew about the magical town of Brockton and its famous visitor. Department

store Santas proliferated and in the early twentieth century red suits for Santas were being sold by Sears Roebuck.

Santa gradually acquired traditions uniquely his own. During the nineteeth century, children mailed letters to their special benefactor, some addressed simply to "Santa Claus." In the 1890s the post office began the practice of making the letters of less fortunate children available to generous-hearted citizens. Snacks for Santa became customary sometime around the beginning of this century. And, of course, children still sit on Santa's knee at department stores across the country, answering the same question asked of them for centuries: "Have you been a good little girl (or boy)?"

One hundred sixty-eight years is not a long life-span for a legend. In our world, where change leaves us breathless, we might wonder how Santa Claus will prosper in future generations. Yet who among us doubts that as long as charity, generosity, and love for children is celebrated, Santa will live on? We need only look at any bright-eyed five-year-old on Christmas morning to know Santa's future is assured.

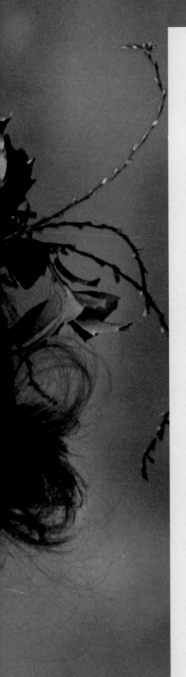

Palace of St. Nicholas
In the Moon
Christmas Morning

My dear Susie Clemens:

I have received and read all the letters which you and your little sister
have written me by the hand of your mother and your nurses; I have also
read those which you little people have written me with your own hands—
for although you did not use any characters that are in grown peoples'
alphabet, you used the characters that all children in all lands on earth and
in the twinkling stars use; and as all my subjects in the moon are children
and use no character but that, you will easily understand that I can read
your and your baby sister's jagged and fantastic marks without any trouble
at all. But I had trouble with those letters which you dictated through your
mother and the nurses, for I am a foreigner and cannot read English writ-
ing well. You will find that I made no mistakes about the things which you
and the baby ordered in your *own* letters—I went down your chimney at
midnight when you were asleep and delivered them all myself—and
kissed both of you, too, because you are good children, well-trained, nice-
mannered, and about the most obedient little people I ever saw. But in the
letters which you dictated there were some words which I could not make
out for certain, and one or two small orders which I could not fill because
we ran out of stock. Our last lot of kitchen-furniture for dolls has just gone
to a very poor little child in the North Star away up in the cold country
above the Big Dipper. Your mama can show you that star and you will say:
"Little Snow Flake" (for that is the child's name), "I'm glad you got that
furniture, for you need it more than I." That is, you must *write* that, with
your own hand, and Snow Flake will write you an answer. If you only
spoke it she wouldn't hear you. Make your letter light and thin, for the
distance is great and the postage very heavy.

Your loving
SANTA CLAUS

*[Samuel Clemens, a.k.a. Mark Twain]*

# Christmas
# Within the Heart

# Is There a Santa Claus?

*Even in the age of Victoria, skepticism tinged the innocence of childhood. In 1897, Virginia O'Hanlon sought the truth from the only source she trusted, THE NEW YORK SUN:*

Dear Editor:

I am 8 years old.

Some of my little friends say there is no Santa Claus. Papa says "If you see it in *The Sun,* it's so." Please tell me the truth, is there a Santa Claus?

Virginia O'Hanlon
115 West 95th Street
New York City.

*Francis Church, the son of a Baptist minister, graduate of Columbia College, and Civil War correspondent, reluctantly took the assignment. His editorial response is, perhaps, the most famous ever written.*

Virginia, your little friends are wrong. They have been affected by the skepticism of a skeptical age. They do not believe except they see. They think that nothing can be which is not comprehensible by their little minds. All minds, Virginia, whether they be men's or children's, are little. In this great universe of ours man is a mere insect, an ant, in his intellect as compared with the boundless world about him, as measured by the intelligence capable of grasping the whole of truth and knowledge.

Yes, Virginia, there is a Santa Claus. He exists as certainly as love and generosity and devotion exist, and you know that they abound and give to your life its highest beauty and joy. Alas! how dreary would be the world if there were no Santa Claus!

It would be as dreary as if there were no Virginias. There would be no childlike faith, then, no poetry, no romance to make tolerable this existence. We should have no enjoyment except in sense and sight. The external light with which childhood fills the world would be extinguished.

Not believe in Santa Claus! You might as well not believe in fairies! You might get your papa to hire men to watch in all the chimneys on Christmas Eve to catch Santa Claus, but even if they did not see Santa Claus coming down, what would that prove? Nobody sees Santa Claus, but that is no sign that there is no Santa Claus. The most real things in the world are those that neither children nor men can see. Did you ever see fairies dancing on the lawn? Of course not, but that's no proof that they are not there. Nobody can conceive or imagine all the wonders that are unseen or unseeable in the world.

You tear apart the baby's rattle to see what makes the noise inside, but there is a veil covering the unseen world which not the strongest man, not even the united strength of all the strongest men that ever lived can tear apart. Only faith, fancy, poetry, love, romance, can push aside that curtain and view and picture the supernal beauty and glory beyond. Is it all real? Ah, Virginia, in all this world there is nothing else real and abiding.

No Santa Claus! Thank God he lives, and he lives forever. A thousand years from now, Virginia, nay, ten times ten thousand years from now, he will continue to make glad the heart of childhood.

*Francis Church died in 1906. THE NEW YORK SUN ceased publication in 1950. Virginia O'Hanlon died in 1971 at the age of eighty-two. Truths of the heart live forever.*

# Angel Candle Holder

*A vigilant angel lights the way for the peace and joy of Christmas into your home. Simple hues, a rustic cut, and a single candle all lend their spartan charm to this folk art treasure.*

## SIZE

Finished candle holder, 8¼" high.

## EQUIPMENT

Pencil. Ruler. Tracing paper. Carbon paper. Strong clamp or vise. Hack saw. Fret saw. Drill, with brace and ⅝" bit. Hammer. Wood glue. Masking tape. Sable brushes, large and fine, for painting with acrylics. Wide, flat brush, for varnish. Medium- and fine-grade sandpaper. Tack cloth. Flat and rounded sanding blocks.

## MATERIALS

Fir or pine, planed and ready for use: ¾"-thick, piece 9" × 4"; ⅜"-thick piece, 20" × 4". Wood nail, 1¼". Acrylic paints, white and gold. Matte varnish.

## DIRECTIONS

**To Cut Out Pieces**: Trace body pattern; transfer to ¾"-thick wood, using carbon paper and pencil; use ruler for straight lines; make sure foot bottom is straight, because overall balance of candle holder depends on straightness of base. Secure marked wood in place on table, using clamp or vise; cut base line and any other straight lines with hack saw. Use fret saw for finer curves. Reserve wood scraps.

Cut ⅜"-thick wood in half to form two 10" × 4" pieces; bind wood halves firmly together, using masking tape. Trace wing and arm patterns; transfer to doubled wood following original patterns for placement on straight grain. Clamp wood securely in place; cut out arms and wings. Reserve wood scraps.

Trace and transfer flower-shaped candle base top to remaining ⅜"-thick wood. Secure wood to table, placing wood scrap underneath area to be drilled. (This will help prevent wood from splitting.) Use brace and drill to make ⅝"-diameter hole in center of flower shape, drilling completely through wood. Cut out flower shape, using fret saw. On scrap of ¾"-thick wood, mark 1½" × ¾" rectangle, for bottom of candle base. Cut out rectangle to form cube, making sure that cut sides are at right angles to top and bottom surfaces. On two opposite 1½" × ¾" surfaces, mark diago-nal lines, using pencil, to locate center of each. Drill hole in center of one marked surface (cube top) to depth of ¼". Hammer

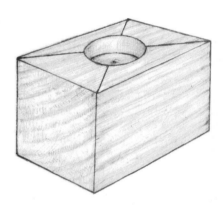

wood nail into cube bottom at marked center so that nail protrudes through center of drilled hole on top. (Nail will secure base of candle when inserted into holder.)

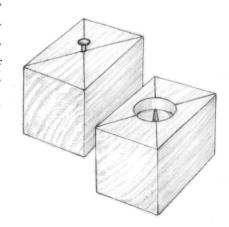

28

Sand surfaces and edges of cube and flower-shaped base top, using flat and rounded sanding blocks as necessary. Sand along grain of wood wherever possible. Sand arms and wings in same manner, making sure that palms of hands are flat. Sand angel body, making sure that feet are level. Dust with tack cloth.

**To Paint**: Using large sable brush and white paint, paint cube and dress, covering both sides of body and leaving head and neck unpainted. Paint arms white down to wrist, leaving hands and inside surfaces of arms unpainted. Paint hair, wings, feet, and sides and top of flower-shaped candle base top, using gold.

When body is dry, use fine brush and gold paint to mark decorative lines and dots on dress; see color photograph. If necessary, paint details twice, to strengthen designs. Let all paint dry thoroughly, at least overnight.

**To Assemble**: Glue pieces together as directed; let glue dry thoroughly after each step before proceeding to next step: Glue flower-shaped candle base top to cube bottom, matching up drill holes. Glue hands to cube:

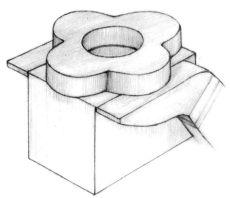

Place hands parallel to and just underneath bottom of base top; use scrap piece of ¾″-thick wood as spacer at shoulder end, to keep arms parallel and uniformly distanced. When hands are firmly attached and glue is dry, glue arms to body, referring to dash lines on original pattern for placement. Test-fit wings

against body and hold in place with masking tape to mark placement. Positioning of wings is crucial to balancing body, so mark gluing line carefully on each side of body. Glue wings in place on body. As with arms, use scrap piece of ¾″-thick wood as spacer while glue dries.

**To Finish**: Let assembled angel dry for at least 12 hours, then coat evenly with matte varnish; let dry, then apply second coat over first.

## SAFETY TIP

Candle holder is made of wood and will ignite if candle is allowed to burn all the way down. REMEMBER: NEVER LEAVE A BURNING CANDLE UNATTENDED!

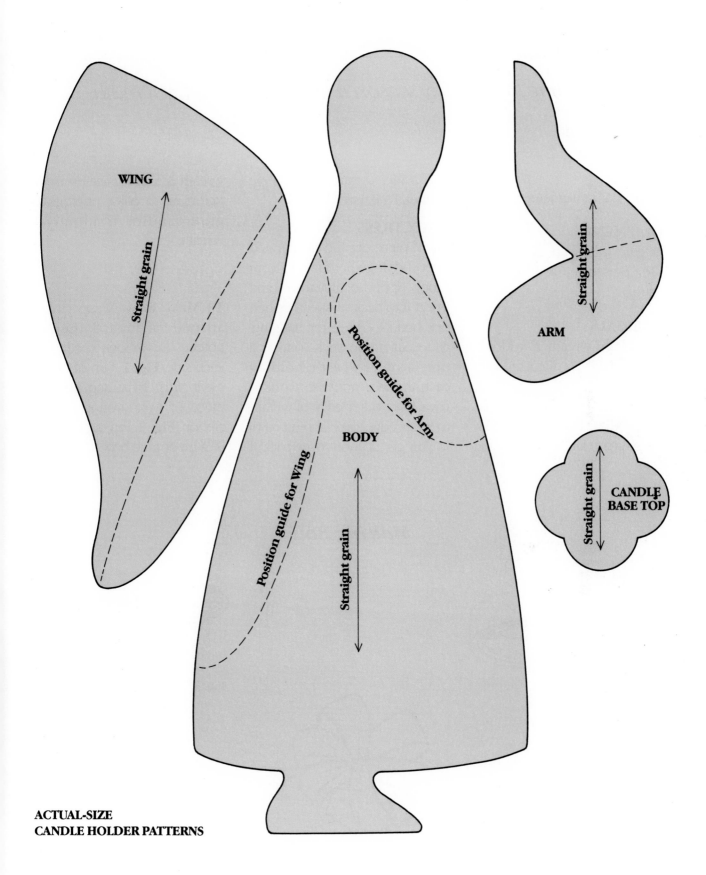

WING

Straight grain

Position guide for Arm

Position guide for Wing

BODY

Straight grain

ARM

Straight grain

Straight grain

CANDLE
BASE TOP

**ACTUAL-SIZE
CANDLE HOLDER PATTERNS**

# Cinnamon Stick Wreath

*Welcome the holiday season with this sweet, spicy wreath.*

**SIZE**
About 13½" in diameter.

**EQUIPMENT**
Hot-glue gun with glue sticks. Ruler. Scissors. Cardboard, 8" wide.

**MATERIALS**
Plastic foam wreath 2" wide, 2" thick, and 12" in diameter. Cinnamon sticks 2"-3" long, about 2½ lbs. Red/white peppermint hard candies, 1" in diameter, 19. Red gingham lace-edged ribbon 1¾" wide, 2 yards long. Pipe cleaner. Fine wire.

**DIRECTIONS**
Cut 4" piece of pipe cleaner and twist ends together for 1" to form a loop. Apply hot glue to end and insert into back of wreath; when dry, bend loop up for hanging. Glue cinnamon sticks one at a time around wreath, holding each in place until set; work in rows from outer edge of wreath to inner edge, overlapping rows as you go; do not cover back if wreath is to hang against a wall. Referring to color photograph, glue candies randomly to wreath.

**To Make Bow**: Wrap ribbon around cardboard, then cut notches in ribbons at center of each side, **Fig. 1**. Slip ribbon off cardboard. Twist and tighten a piece of wire around notched ribbon, **Fig. 2**. Fan out bow, **Fig. 3**. Wire or glue bow to wreath.

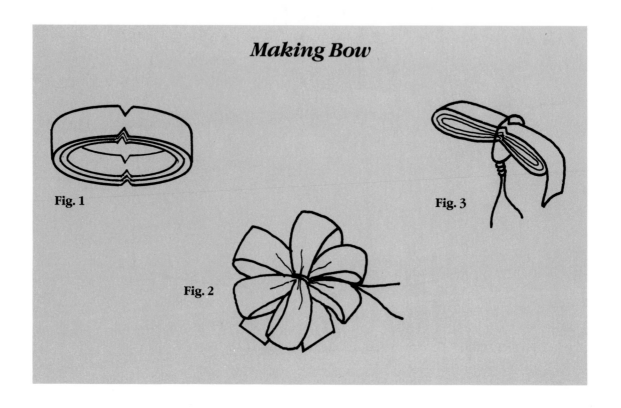

**Making Bow**

Fig. 1

Fig. 2

Fig. 3

# Candles in the Dark

Her bowl is washed and sits on a shelf. Her favorite grass green rug is also clean and stored, for what future use I don't know. Her favorite large rock sits at the edge of the driveway, as if waiting for familiar paws and jaws to push it around for hours on end.

Sigi, our silver German Shepherd with the beautiful markings on her face, has been gone for four holiday seasons now, but her presence is still felt. Sometimes I think I "see" her at her favorite spots in the house, especially by the living room window where she'd watch the world go by. At other times, especially when rising in the morning, I expect to see her on the floor by my bed — smiling, on her back, feet up in the air, waiting for me to scratch her belly.

And hugs. How she loved hugs!

Sigi died in 1986 from the crippling effects of old age. Toward the end, she couldn't walk or bark. But until the end, she knew she was loved.

In her lifetime, Sigi loved many activities and people, including car rides and Popo, my gentle, good-natured mother-in-law. I occasionally took Sigi along in my old Ford Mustang for visits to Popo's place. Sigi liked to stick her head straight out of the car's sun roof, the wind blowing in her furry face as we zoomed along the highway.

Sigi and Popo got along splendidly. Whenever Sigi rushed toward her to plant a wet kiss on her cheek, Popo would open her eyes wide in mock horror and raise her arms in self defense. "No, no," she'd laugh, thoroughly enjoying the moment.

Popo came to Hawaii from China in the early 1900s as the bride of her Hawaii-born husband. Understandably, she clung to traditional cultural practices and beliefs that gave her great comfort in her new home. On her lanai, she kept a tiny altar that was adorned with an incense burner and a statuette of the Chinese goddess of mercy, Kwan Yin.

Popo made the best "Chinese lemons," which were aged for years in glass jars. "These are hard to get so use them only when you have a cold or are not feeling well," she said, half her words coming out in Chinese, the other half in English.

Sick or not, I always found excuses to eat the

tangy, shrunken lemons like snacks. I'd put my hand on my throat, cough a little and say, "Maybe I'm coming down with something." Popo would look at me knowingly, chuckle, and give me a whole bunch of delicious lemons.

When I worked for an airline, my husband and I lived with Popo for a short while. Anyone else might have found my upside-down routine of sleeping by day, flying by night and eating spaghetti for breakfast rather strange. But Popo took in stride the daughter-in-law who lived in pajamas, who went to work wearing a mini-skirt, fishnet stockings and white Donald Duck cap and who considered noon (or later) the normal time to get up.

Popo's generosity and sweetness of character was especially illuminated during the holiday season when she immersed herself in the spirit of things. Every year, she'd decorate a Christmas tree with angels, shiny ornaments, blinking lights and various knickknacks given to her by her children and grandchildren.

Today, a cheerful Christmas tree no longer lights up Popo's apartment. Like Sigi, she died from the infirmities of old age. Toward the end, she also couldn't walk or talk. That was six Christmases ago, in 1984.

But through their daily examples, Sigi and Popo taught me some enduring lessons — about treasuring the moment, about relationships that really matter, about tolerance and openness, about making sincere efforts. They appreciated, even rejoiced in, simple things, and even during the rough times, their spirits glowed.

I think often of Sigi and Popo. I miss them a lot. With their passing, I've noticed at least one change in my own behavior: In the past I rarely put up a Christmas tree because I usually found an excuse not to have one. "Why bother?" "Too commercialized." "Humbug." You get the picture. But in recent years, a small tree has brightened our living room during the holidays. Like Popo, I decorate it with blinking lights, tinsel, carved wooden animals, porcelain angels, and knickknacks from friends and relatives.

And now, more than ever, I understand why Popo had one.

*Thelma Chang*

# Doughcraft Trims

*Whip up a batch of doughcraft folk art ornaments featuring Star, Heart, and Christmas Tree, or a colorfully festive variety to gaily adorn your tree or Christmas packages.*

# Folk Art Ornaments

## EQUIPMENT

Pencil. Ruler. Tracing paper. White cardboard (posterboard). White glue. Scissors. Sharp knife. Aspic (tiny) cutters: petalled flower, tulip, leaf, and crescent. Fine pointed paintbrushes, for acrylics. Wide, flat brush, for polyurethane. Skewer.

## MATERIALS

Flour/Salt Dough #1 (see recipe). Acrylic paints: white and colors. Polyurethane. Ribbon, cord, or yarn, for hanging loops.

### Flour/Salt Dough #1

4  cups white flour
1  cup salt (iodized or plain)
1½ cups water

In big bowl, mix flour and salt until well-blended and smooth. Add 1 cup water and continue to mix. Slowly add remaining ½ cup water, turning dough in bowl. Push dough into a ball, working in any dry flour and salt left in bottom of bowl. Knead on floured surface for at least 10 minutes. Wrap dough tightly in plastic.

## SPECIAL HINTS

If dough is too dry, wet your hands and continue kneading, working moisture into dough. You may have to repeat this several times; add moisture slowly, or dough may become too moist ("weepy"). If dough is too wet, add ¼ cup flour to ¼ cup salt and dust kneading surface with flour/salt mixture. As you knead, mixture will be incorporated into dough. Continue dusting and kneading until dough is firm.

## ORNAMENTS

Prepare templates: Trace actual-size patterns, using ruler to mark straight edges. Glue tracings to cardboard; let dry. Cut out along outlines; cut away inner heart.

Make dough. Roll out dough for star, heart, and tree (plus branches) on lightly floured surface to ⅛" thickness. Roll out dough for trims to less than ⅛". Cut out ornaments by placing lightly floured templates on rolled-out dough; cut into dough along template edges, using sharp knife. Use aspic cutters to cut out trims. Smooth all cut edges with fingers. Hand-roll tiny amounts of dough to form tiny balls and stems.

*For Star:* Cut out star, 3 flowers, and 6 leaves.

*For Heart:* Cut out heart, 18-20 tulips, 5-6 flowers, and 8-10 leaves.

*For Tree:* Cut out tree, 10 branches, 4 flowers, and 4 crescents. Roll 18 tiny balls and a few thin strands for stems.

Make hole at center top of each ornament for attaching hanging loop (see How-To). Assemble ornaments, arranging dough trims as shown in color photograph, or as desired, before baking. Using skewer, make center hole in each petalled flower; score crescents and center veins of leaves, using sharp knife. Brush ornament front with water; gently press flowers, tulips, crescents, leaves, balls, and stems in place.

Place trimmed ornaments on flour-dusted cookie sheet. Bake at low heat (250°-300°) until hard. Remove ornaments from oven; allow to cool thoroughly. Paint entire ornament with base coat of white acrylic; let dry. Paint ornaments with colors shown or as desired. When paint is dry, brush on several thin coats of polyurethane to seal ornament; let dry thoroughly after applying each coat. To finish ornaments, make and attach hanging loop (see How-To).

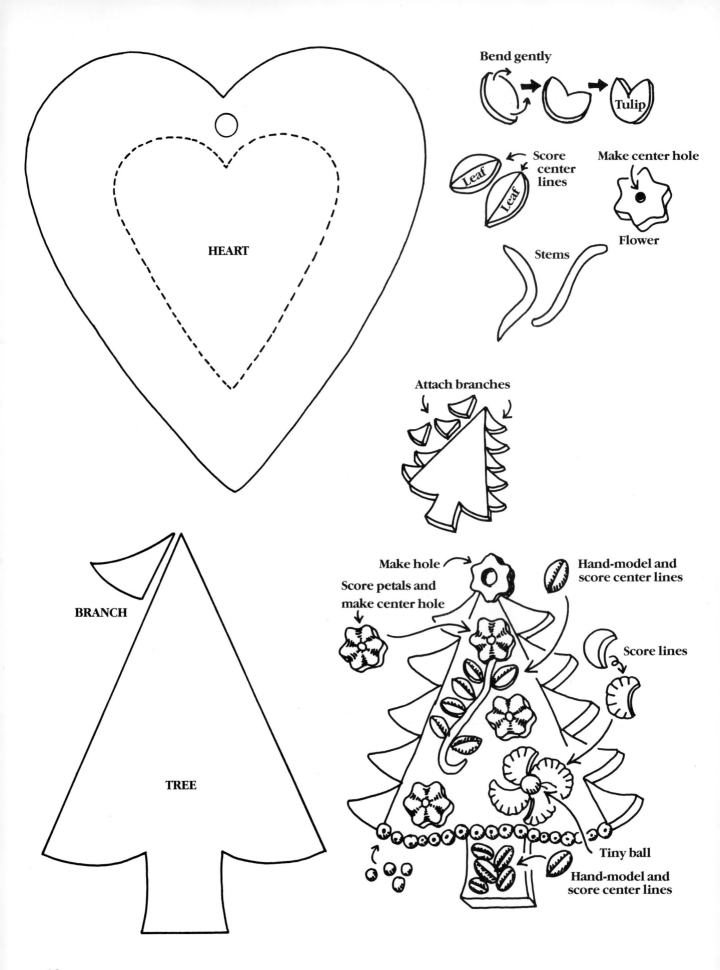

Bend gently

Tulip

Score center lines

Leaf

Leaf

Make center hole

Flower

Stems

HEART

Attach branches

Make hole

Hand-model and score center lines

Score petals and make center hole

Score lines

BRANCH

TREE

Tiny ball

Hand-model and score center lines

## How to Hang an Ornament

### MATERIALS

Narrow ribbons in satin, gros-
grain, velvet, taffeta
Inexpensive ribbons used for
tying packages
Yarns in thick or thin weights,
one or more strands
Plain round and flat cords
Fancy cords like soutache, middy
braid, and rat tail
Metallic gold, silver, and bright-
colored cords and braids
Baby rickrack
Plastic straw
Wooden Skewer
Toothpicks

## TWO WAYS TO MAKE A HOLE

1. Press one end of plastic straw
completely through dough without lifting dough. Withdraw
straw gently, taking excess
dough out with it. If you need
straw to make more holes, be
sure to clean out dough, using
toothpick.

2. Press blunt end of a wooden
skewer through dough without
lifting dough. Make a tiny circular motion with skewer to
enlarge hole as much as necessary. Be sure hole is clean and
goes completely through dough.

## FOUR WAYS TO ATTACH A RIBBON (CORD, YARN, ETC.)

1. Thread ribbon ends through
hole in ornament; tie into bow.
Trim ribbon ends.
2. Slip ribbon loop through
hole. Thread ribbon ends
through loop; tie bow or knot.
3. Glue ribbon ends to back of
ornament.
4. Thread one ribbon end
through hole; tie bow.

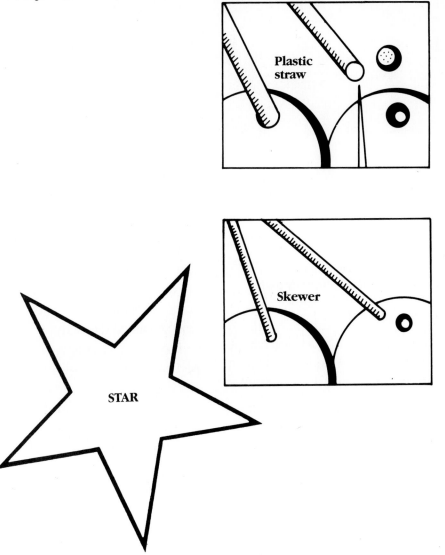

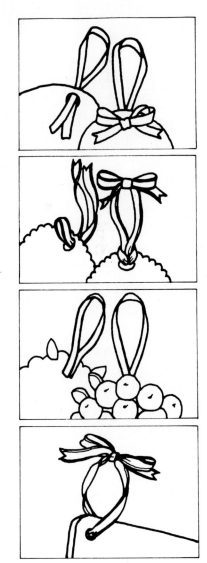

## Bright and Pretty Dough Trims

### EQUIPMENT

Pencil. Ruler. Tracing paper. Compass. Small sharp knife. Toothpicks. Large and small scalloped cookie cutters. Kitchen grater with tiny holes (for Nest ornament only). Fine pointed paintbrushes, for acrylics. Wide, flat brush, for polyurethane.

### MATERIALS

Flour/Salt Dough #2 (see recipe). Acrylic paints: white and colors. Polyurethane. Fine wire, for hanging loops.

### Flour/Salt Dough #2

| | |
|---|---|
| 4 | cups white flour |
| 1 | cup salt (iodized or plain) |
| 2 | tsp. mustard powder |
| 1¼ | cups water |

In big bowl, mix dry ingredients until well-blended and smooth. Add 1 cup water and continue to mix. Slowly add remaining ¼ cup of water, turning dough in bowl. Push dough into a ball, working in any dry ingredients left in bottom of bowl. Knead on floured surface for at least 10 minutes. Wrap dough tightly in plastic.

### DIRECTIONS

Trace actual-size patterns; do not cut out. Patterns indicate general sizes and shapes only and need not be followed exactly.

To make each shape, pinch off piece of clay and roll into ball. Place dough on tracing; flatten and form it into desired shape, using tracing as guide and following individual directions below for suggested thicknesses. Use knife and other small tools (such as for manicuring) as needed to aid in shaping.

TREE

BIRD'S NEST

BELL

SNOWMAN

SANTA HEAD

41

To join pieces (such as for pretzel or wreath), wet fingertip with water and use to moisten shape; press pieces together; see color photograph and individual directions.

Place shapes on flour-dusted cookie sheet for final shaping. When wreaths and ornaments are assembled, form short length of wire into loop; insert wire ends into top of ornament or wreath, for hanging loop. Prick shapes with toothpick in several places, to prevent uneven rising. Bake at low heat (250°-300°) until hard, about 2-3 hours, depending upon thickness of dough. Remove shapes from oven; allow to cool thoroughly.

Paint shape with base coat of white acrylic, leaving tan areas in natural cookie color; let dry. Paint shapes with colors shown or as desired. When paint is dry,

brush on several coats of polyurethane to seal ornament; let dry thoroughly after applying each coat.

## Wreaths

Make number of shapes indicated in individual directions below; form shapes with recommended thicknesses. Use compass to draw two concentric circles on tracing paper, for wreath guide; see individual directions for inner and outer diameters. Moisten shapes and press together. Transfer wreath to cookie sheet; bake and finish.

**Santa Head Wreath** (2″ inner diameter; 8″ outer diameter): Make eight ½″-thick heads. Add ⅛″-thick strip for hatband. Add tiny dot for nose.

**Snowman Wreath** (1½″ inner diameter; 7″ outer diameter): Make nine ⅝″-thick snowmen. Add hatband as for Santa Head

and three ⅛″-thick muffler pieces. Add tiny dot for nose.

**Tree Wreath** (1½″ inner diameter; 9″ outer diameter): Make eight ⅝″-thick trees. Add tiny ⅛″-thick decorations.

## Ornaments

**Pretzel**: From ball, roll 10″ × ½″ coil or dough; twist into pretzel shape.

**Bell**: Form ½″-thick bell. Add ⅛″-thick bow pieces.

**Bird's Nest**: Flatten dough to ¼″ thickness × 2¾″ diameter. For nest, push dough through grater and arrange on dough, for "twigs." Make ¼″-thick bird and eggs.

**Scalloped Wreath**: Flatten dough to ¼″-⅜″ thickness. Use cookie cutters to cut out shapes. Add ⅛″-thick birds, or sprinkle dough with sesame seeds.

# Patchwork Ornaments

*Fill these patchwork ornaments with potpourri*
*to create sweet-smelling Christmas tree decorations.*

## SIZE

Each ornament, 3″ square.

## EQUIPMENT

Pencil. Ruler. Tracing and graph paper. Thin, stiff cardboard. Glue. Scissors. Straight pins. Sewing needle. Large-eyed embroidery needle. Sewing machine. Iron. Knitting needle.

## MATERIALS

Closely woven cotton fabric scraps of the following colors and patterns: red solid; white-on-red dotted; red print; light, medium, and dark green solids; light green print; ecru solid; ecru print. Sewing threads to match fabrics. Cotton cording 1/16″ diameter, 1½ yards red. Polyester fiberfill or cotton balls.

## GENERAL DIRECTIONS

Mark patterns on graph paper, following individual directions below. Glue graph paper to cardboard; let dry; cut carefully along marked lines for templates. Use templates to mark

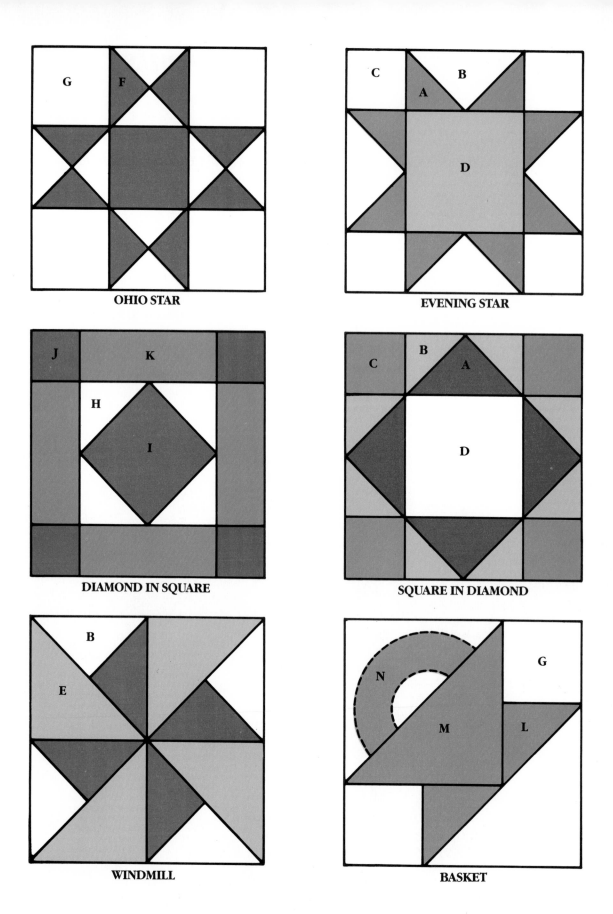

**OHIO STAR**

**EVENING STAR**

**DIAMOND IN SQUARE**

**SQUARE IN DIAMOND**

**WINDMILL**

**BASKET**

44

pieces as directed: Place template on wrong side of fabric with right angles, two parallel edges, or one straight edge on straight of goods. Draw around template with sharp pencil held at an outward angle. Mark as many pieces as needed of one color at a time, leaving ½" between two pieces. Cut out pieces ¼" outside pencil lines for seam allowance; pencil lines will be stitching lines. To join two pieces, place them together with right sides facing, matching one edge; stitch on marked line; press seam to one side, under darker color. Join pieces to form a block 3½" square, following individual directions, diagrams, and color photograph.

**To Assemble** (for each): Cut 3½" fabric square for back. Pin patchwork front and back together, wrong sides out; stitch ¼" from edges all around, leaving 2" opening in one edge; turn to right side. Stuff until plump, poking stuffing into corners with knitting needle. Turn raw edge ¼" to inside; slip-stitch opening closed. **For hanging loop:** From cording, cut 9" length. Use embroidery needle to thread cord through one corner (top) of ornament; remove needle and knot ends together.

### Evening Star
(middle right, in photograph): Read General Directions above. Make templates: Divide a ¾" square in half diagonally for triangle shape and label it A. Divide a 1¹⁄₁₆" square in half diagonally for triangle B. For C, make a ¾" square. For D, make a 1½" square. From solid dark green fabric, cut eight of A. From solid ecru fabric, cut four each of B and C. From green print fabric, cut one of D.

Following diagram, join A's to B's. Join C's to two A-B-A pieces. Join third and fourth A-B-A pieces to D. Join pieces as shown, completing block. Assemble ornament and attach hanging loop, following General Directions.

### Square in Diamond
(bottom left, in photograph): Read General Directions above. Make templates for A, B, C, and D: See directions above for Evening Star. From solid dark green fabric, cut eight of A. From solid red fabric, cut four of B. From green print fabric, cut four of C. From solid light green fabric, cut one of D.

Following diagram, join pieces to form block as directed for Evening Star, except reversing position of A-B-A pieces as shown. Assemble ornament and attach hanging loop, following General Directions.

### Windmill
(top left, in photograph): Read General Directions above. Make template for B: See directions above for Evening Star. Divide a 1½" square in half diagonally for triangle E. From red print and dotted fabrics, cut four each of B. From solid medium green fabric, cut four of E.

Following diagram, join B's at short edges. Join B-B pieces to long edge of E's. Join B-B-E pieces as shown, completing block. Assemble ornament and attach hanging loop, following General Directions.

### Ohio Star
(top right, in photograph): Read General Directions above. Make templates: Divide a 1" square in quarters diagonally for triangle shape and label it F. For G, make a 1" square. From solid ecru fabric, cut eight of F and four of G. From solid red fabric, cut one of G and eight of F.

Following diagram, join F's. Join G's to F's as shown to form three strips. Join strips, completing block. Assemble ornament and attach hanging loop, following General Directions.

### Diamond in Square
(bottom right, in photograph): Read General Directions above. Make templates: Divide a ⅞" square in half diagonally for triangle shape and label it H. For I, make a 1¼" square. For J, make a ⅝" square. For K, make a 1¾" × ⅝" rectangle. From solid light green fabric, cut four of H. From red dotted fabric, cut one of I and four of J. From solid dark green fabric, cut four of K.

Following diagram, join H's to I. Join J's to ends of two K's. Join third and fourth K's to H's. Join pieces as shown, completing block. Assemble ornament and attach hanging loop, following General Directions.

## Basket

(middle left, in photograph): Read General Directions above. Make template for G: See directions above for Ohio Star. Divide G in half diagonally for triangle L. Divide a 2″ square in half diagonally for triangle M. Trace actual size pattern N and make template. From ecru print fabric, cut two each of G and M. From solid dark green fabric, cut two of L and one of M; also cut one of N, referring to instructions for appliqué (see page 81).

Following diagram, join G's to L's. Following directions for hand-appliqué, pin, baste, and stitch N to one ecru print M, with straight edges even and side margins equal; see dash lines on diagram. Attach M's as shown, completing block. Assemble ornament and attach hanging loop, following General Directions above.

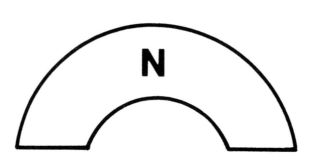

# The Tree That Didn't Get Trimmed

*All young fir trees dream of being a Christmas Tree someday.
But every December there are more trees cut down
than are needed for Christmas.*

If you walk through a grove of balsam trees you will notice that the young trees are silent; they are listening. But the old tall ones—especially the firs—are whispering. They are telling the story of The Tree That Didn't Get Trimmed. It sounds like a painful story, and the murmur of the old trees as they tell it is rather solemn; but it is an encouraging story for young saplings to hear. On warm autumn days when your trunk is tickled by ants and insects climbing, and the resin is hot and gummy in your knots, and the whole glade smells sweet, drowsy, and sad, and the hardwood trees are boasting of the gay colours they are beginning to show, many a young evergreen has been cheered by it.

All young fir trees, as you know by that story of Hans Andersen's—if you've forgotten it, why not read it again?—dream of being a Christmas Tree some day. They dream about it as young girls dream of being a bride, or young poets of having a volume of verse published. With the vision of that brightness and gayety before them they patiently endure the sharp sting of the ax, the long hours pressed together on a freight car. But every December there are more trees cut down than are needed for Christmas. And that is the story that no one—not even Hans Andersen—has thought to put down.

The tree in this story should never have been cut. He wouldn't have been, but it was getting dark in the Vermont woods, and the man with the ax said to himself, "Just one more." Cutting young trees with a sharp, beautifully balanced ax is fascinating; you go on and on; there's a sort of cruel pleasure in it. The blade goes through the soft wood with one whistling stroke and the boughs sink down with a soft swish.

He was a fine, well-grown youngster, but too tall for his age; his branches were rather scraggly. If he'd been left there he would have been an unusually big tree some day; but now he was in the awkward age and didn't have the tapering shape and the thick, even foliage that people like on Christmas trees. Worse still, instead of running up to a straight, clean spire, his top was a bit lopsided, with a fork in it.

But he didn't know this as he stood with many others, leaning against the side wall of the green-grocer's shop. In those cold December days he was very happy, thinking of the pleasures to come. He had heard of the delights of Christmas Eve: the stealthy setting-up of the tree, the tinsel balls and coloured toys and stars, the peppermint canes and birds with spun-glass tails. Even that old anxiety of Christmas trees—burning candles—did not worry him, for he had been told that nowadays people use strings of tiny electric bulbs which cannot set one on fire. So he looked forward to the festival with a confident heart.

"I shall be very grand," he said. "I hope there will be children to admire me. It must be a great moment when the children hang their stockings on you!" He even felt sorry for the first trees that were chosen and taken away. It would be best, he considered, not to be bought until Christmas Eve. Then, in the shining darkness someone would pick him out, put him carefully along the running board of a car, and away they would go. The tire-chains would clack and jingle merrily on the snowy road. He imagined a big house with fire glowing on a hearth; the hushed rustle of wrapping paper and parcels being unpacked. Someone would say, "Oh, what a beautiful tree!" How erect and stiff he would brace himself in his iron tripod stand.

But day after day went by, one by one the other trees were taken, and he began to grow troubled. For everyone who looked at him seemed to have an unkind word. "Too tall," said one lady. "No, this one wouldn't do, the branches are too skimpy," said another. "If I chop off the top," said the green-grocer, "it wouldn't be so bad?" The tree shuddered, but the customer had already passed on to look at others. Some of his branches ached where the grocer had bent them upward to make his shape more attractive.

Across the street was a Ten Cent Store. Its bright windows were full of scarlet odds and ends; when the doors opened he could see people crowded along the aisles, cheerfully jostling one another with bumpy packages. A buzz of talk, a shuffle of feet, a constant ringing of cash drawers came noisily out of that doorway. He could see flashes of marvellous colour, ornaments for luckier trees. Every evening, as the time drew nearer, the pavements were more thronged. The handsomer trees, not so tall as he but more bushy and shapely, were ranked in front of him; as they were taken away he could see the gayety only too well. Then he was shown to a lady who wanted a tree very cheap. "You can have this one for a dollar," said the grocer. This was only one-third of what the grocer had asked for him at first, but even so the lady refused him and went across the street to buy a little artificial tree at the toy store. The man pushed him back carelessly, and he toppled over and fell alongside the wall. No one bothered to pick him up. He was almost glad, for now his pride would be spared.

ow it was Christmas Eve. It was a foggy evening with a drizzling rain; the alley alongside the store was thick with trampled slush. As he lay there among broken boxes and fallen scraps of holly strange thoughts came to him. In the still northern forest already his wounded stump was buried in forgetful snow. He remembered the wintry sparkle of the woods, the big trees with crusts and clumps of silver on their broad boughs, the keen singing of the lonely wind. He remembered the strong, warm feeling of his roots reaching down into the safe earth. That is a good feeling; it means to a tree just what it means to you to stretch your toes down toward the bottom of a well-tucked bed. And he had given up all this to lie here, disdained and forgotten, in a littered alley. The splash of feet, the chime of bells, the cry of cars went past him. He trembled a little with self-pity and vexation. "No toys and stockings for me," he thought sadly, and shed some of his needles.

Late that night, after all the shopping was over, the grocer came out to clear away what was left. The boxes, the broken wreaths, the empty barrels, and our tree with one or two others that hadn't been sold, all were thrown through the side door into the cellar. The door was locked and he lay there in the dark. One of his branches, doubled under him in the fall, ached so he thought it must be broken. "So this is Christmas," he said to himself.

ll that day it was still in the cellar. There was an occasional creak as one of the bruised trees tried to stretch itself. Feet went along the pavement overhead, and there was a booming of church bells, but everything had a slow, disappointed sound. Christmas is always a little sad, after such busy preparations. The unwanted trees lay on the stone floor, watching the furnace light flicker on a hatchet that had been left there.

The day after Christmas a man came in who wanted some green boughs to decorate a cemetery. The grocer took the hatchet, and seized the trees without ceremony. They were too disheartened to care. Chop, chop, chop, went the blade, and the sweet-smelling branches were carried away. The naked trunks were thrown into a corner.

And now our tree, what was left of him, had plenty of time to think. He no longer could feel anything, for trees feel with their branches, but they think with their trunks. What did he think about as he grew dry and stiff? He thought that it had been silly of him to imagine such a fine, gay career for himself, and he was sorry for other young trees, still growing in the fresh hilly country, who were enjoying the same fantastic dreams.

Now perhaps you don't know what happens to the trunks of leftover Christmas trees. You could never guess. Farmers come in from the suburbs and buy them at five cents each for bean-poles and grape arbors. So perhaps (here begins the encouraging part of this story) they are really happier, in the end, than the trees that get trimmed for Santa Claus. They go back into the fresh moist earth of spring, and when the sun grows hot the quick tendrils of the vines climb up them and presently they are decorated with the red blossoms of the bean or the little blue globes of the grape, just as pretty as any Christmas trinkets.

So one day the naked, dusty fir-poles were taken out of the cellar, and thrown into a truck with many others, and made a rattling journey out into the land. The farmer unloaded them in his yard and was stacking them up by the barn when his wife came out to watch him.

"There!" she said. "That's just what I want, a nice long pole with a fork in it. Jim, put that one over there to hold up the clothesline." It was the first time that anyone had praised our tree, and his dried-up heart swelled with a tingle of forgotten sap. They put him near one end of the clothesline, with his stump close to a flower bed. The fork that had been despised for a Christmas star was just the thing to hold up a clothesline. It was a washday, and soon the farmer's wife began bringing out wet garments to swing and freshen in the clean bright air. And the very first thing that hung near the top of the Christmas pole was a cluster of children's stockings.

That isn't quite the end of the story, as the old fir trees whisper it in the breeze. The Tree That Didn't Get Trimmed was so cheerful watching the stockings, and other gay little clothes that plumped out in the wind just as though waiting to be spanked, that he didn't notice what was going on—or going up—below him. A vine had caught hold of his trunk and was steadily twisting upward. And one morning, when the farmer's wife came out intending to shift him, she stopped and exclaimed. "Why, I musn't move this pole," she said. "The morning glory has run right up it." So it had, and our bare pole was blue and crimson with colour.

Something nice, the old firs believe, always happens to the trees that don't get trimmed. They even believe that some day one of the Christmas-tree bean-poles will be the starting-point for another Magic Beanstalk, as in the fairy tale of the boy who climbed up the bean-tree and killed the giant. When that happens, fairy tales will begin all over again.

*Christopher Morley*

# Small Heart Wreaths

*Celebrate this season of love with these sweet
and simple holiday hearts.*

## EQUIPMENT
Wire cutters. Scissors. White glue.

## MATERIALS
Chenille stems. Sheet moss. Spool of very fine wire.

**For Wreath with Berries:** Grosgrain ribbon ⅛″ wide, 15″. Wired berries, 22-25 units.

**For Wreath with Flowers:** Plaid taffeta ribbon ⁵⁄₁₆″ wide, 12″. Dried white statice or similar small flowers, 2-3 stems. Green thread or thin cord.

**For Wreath with Pinecones:** Plaid taffeta ribbon ⁵⁄₁₆″ wide, 10″. Tiny pinecones ½″-¾″ high, 6-8 cones. Small dried yellow flowers with rigid stems, about 40 flowers.

## BASIC HEART WREATH
Bend chenille stem into heart shape, as shown below, twisting ends together at bottom of heart. (Top of heart will be shaped into a point later.)

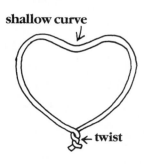

shallow curve

← twist

Cut two strips of sheet moss, each about 8″ × 2″. Cut 24″ length of wire. Beginning at heart bottom, position moss lengthwise along heart side, letting it overhang heart bottom about 1″; wrap moss tightly around chenille; wrap wire firmly around moss to secure in place.

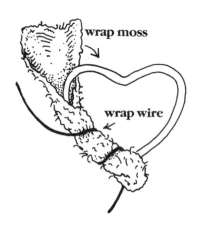

wrap moss

wrap wire

Continue wrapping moss and wire completely around heart, working around top and second side and ending at heart bottom. When first strip of moss is almost used up, overlap end with second moss strip and continue attaching. If wire runs out, cut additional 24″ length; twist one end of new length to end of old length and continue wrapping.

At heart bottom, overlap moss ends for 1″-2″; cut away excess. Wrap wire around moss ends; twist wire ends together tightly on back of heart. Clip away excess wire.

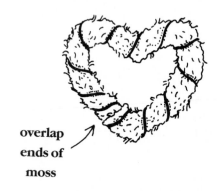

overlap ends of moss

Shape heart top into a more pronounced point. Use scissors to trim heart, just a little, to neaten. Clip off any bits of moss that are sticking out, so that heart shape is defined clearly. Decorate hearts as directed below.

To finish, tie ribbon to heart top to form hanging loop if desired, or connect hearts with wire to form large wreath as shown.

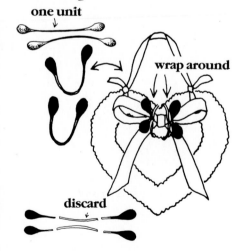

### Wreath with Berries

Tie taffeta ribbon into bow about 3″ wide with ends about 2½″-3″ long (see How to Tie a Bow). Trim ribbon ends on the diagonal. Arrange bow on front of heart. Take two wired berry units and form each into a U-shape; wrap around heart, one on each side of center knot of bow. Twist berries and wire to secure bow in place on heart.

Using wirecutters, clip 12-14 berry units into shorter pieces, discarding extra wire.

Dip wire end of each berry into glue, then insert it into moss around bow as shown in color drawing.

### Wreath with Statice Flowers

Cut dried statice into individual flowers, leaving a little green stem on each flower.

Cut length of green thread and tie it to left side of heart top as shown. Center a flower on thread and wind thread over flower to secure it in place on heart. Arrange a second flower to overlap the first; wind thread around and over second flower to secure it.

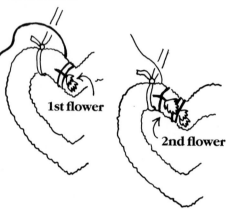

Continue in this manner, working down left half of heart, stopping at heart bottom. Let excess thread hang freely for now. Repeat process to cover right half of heart. At heart bottom, thread ends together securely on back of heart; clip away excess thread.

Tie taffeta ribbon into a bow, snip ends into points, and glue bow to heart as shown in color drawing.

### Wreath with Pinecones

Cut wire length about 8″ long. Wrap one wire end around "petals" at base of one pinecone several times; wire should be securely attached. Wrap free wire end around a second pine-cone, with 2½″-3″ of wire between the pinecones. Repeat with a second pair of pinecones.

Twist wired pinecones together with three berry units. Bend them into a "U" shape; twist around heart top, making cluster.

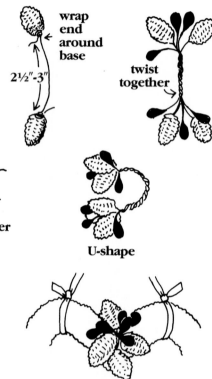

Strip petals from bottom half of each of the remaining 2—4 pinecones, leaving stems exposed. Dip each stem into glue and insert it into moss at one upper curve of heart, at lower point, and so on.

With wirecutters, snip remaining berry units into shorter lengths, discarding excess wire. Break off stem of each dried flower to about ¾″ long.

Tuck berries and flowers around the cluster and down sides of heart as shown; dip each wire or stem into glue and gently insert it into moss.

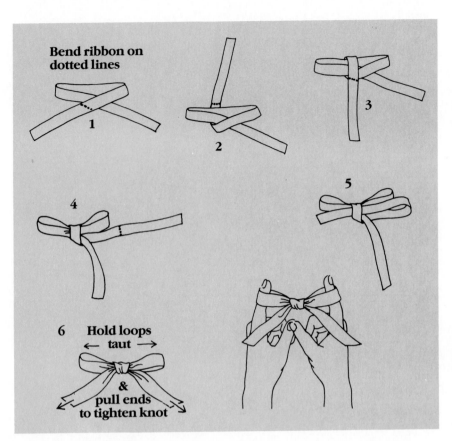

**Bend ribbon on dotted lines**

1

2

3

4

5

6 **Hold loops ← taut →**

**& pull ends to tighten knot**

## HOW TO TIE A BOW

Many ornaments call for a simple, pretty bow that is made from a separate piece of braid or ribbon (any width) and attached with glue. To make this bow, follow step-by-step instructions above, referring to illustrations.

Remember to keep loops taut as you knot the center and be sure to make center knot good and tight. If ribbon has right and wrong sides (like single-face satin ribbon), turn ribbon when necessary to keep right side toward you. When bow is complete, clip ends in single or double points as shown or as desired.

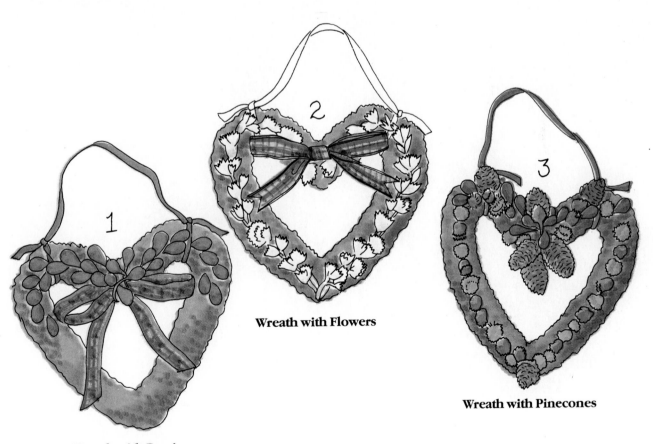

**Wreath with Berries**

**Wreath with Flowers**

**Wreath with Pinecones**

# Bittersweet Christmas

Christmas was the most special holiday of all for my father. The preparations, gift-buying, and decorating were no trouble to him — he enjoyed it all.

Mother told me that he introduced me to my first Christmas tree when I was nine days old. It was a small tree, but every ornament, candle, and strand of silver tinsel was meticulously hung in place, as only he could do it. When he had finally finished, he took me from my bassinet and held me up to see his handiwork.

Daddy lived long enough to decorate just four more Christmas trees — each one a little larger than the year before.

The year he died — after a short bout with pneumonia — Mother sat down with me for a talk about Christmas. "Madeline," she said gently, "Santa will be leaving gifts for you, but we won't be having a tree and decorations. It's just to much to do this year."

The morning of Christmas Eve arrived with no special arrangements for the next day, other than early mass and dinner at a relative's house. Just before noon the phone rang and Mother answered. After a pause, I heard her say, "That's very kind of you, but I think we'll spend the evening here together. It's the first since..." She recovered, thanked the caller again and hung up.

Who was it?" I asked.

"One of our neighbors," Mother said. "She wanted us to come down this evening. I...I can't."

Mother was silent most of the day. Late in the afternoon, she changed her mind. She called our neighbor and told her we'd stop in for a few minutes.

"It's thoughtful of her," Mother said to me, "and we don't want to seem ungrateful."

When we rang the neighbor's doorbell, she kissed us and led us through the foyer. The living room beyond seemed dark with an odd-colored glow. She motioned us forward, and I stepped into the room and caught my breath. There, shining with colored lights and ornaments and gaily wrapped packages, was a magnificent Christmas tree. Seated around it, smiling broadly, were Mrs. Abrams, Mrs. Cohen, Mrs. Blount, Mrs. Dreyfus. "Surprise, surprise!" they chorused.

Today I can close my eyes and bring back that scene at will. Many times it has sustained me when things have gone badly, when I have doubted the human heart. I can still feel the love of those neighbors — those Jewish women who ventured into an unfamiliar tradition so that one little Christian girl without a daddy could have a merry Christmas.

*Madeline Weatherford*

# Nativity Tree Skirt

*Black braid and brilliant colors give this Nativity scene a stained glass look. And because everything is pressed and glued into place, it's extra easy and quick to make.*

**SIZE**

Tree skirt, 55″ diameter.

**EQUIPMENT**

Pencil. Ruler. Paper for patterns. String and thumbtack, for compass. Scissors. Straight pins. Knitting needle. Fabric glue or hot-glue gun with glue sticks.

**MATERIALS**

Medium- or heavy-weight felt 60″ wide, 1⅝ yards; two 9″×12″ rectangles yellow; one 9″×12″ rectangle each of cream, beige, dark brown, red, maroon, dark blue, dark green, emerald, gray, and purple; scraps of pink, orange, gold, dark gold, tan, brown, light blue, and turquoise. Flexible wool braid 1″ wide, 6½ yards each red and green. Black soutache or similar narrow braid trim ⅛″ wide, 11 yards.

**SPECIAL HINT**

Sheets of blue graph or quadrille paper can be purchased at art supply stores, and some sewing stores sell a special 1″ grid paper made for enlarging patterns.

## DIRECTIONS

**To Prepare Tree Skirt**: Make tree-skirt half-pattern: Cut paper at least 56″ × 28″, or tape smaller pieces of paper together to make this size. Mark line entire length of paper ½″ from one long edge; mark center point of line. Prepare a compass by tying knot in one end of string, securing knot to center point with thumbtack and tying other end of string around pencil, leaving 27½″ (radius of circle) between pencil and tack. Draw semicircle on paper with marked straight line as diameter. Using marked center point, draw semicircle with 4″ radius inside large one. Cut out skirt half-pattern along straight edge and inner and outer arcs. Fold white felt in half widthwise; pin pattern in place on doubled felt with straight edge even with fold; trace inner and outer skirt edges. Cut out skirt on marked arcs. With felt still doubled, cut slit between arcs (for center back opening of skirt), using fold as guide.

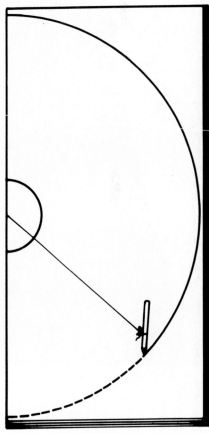

**Marking felt circle**

57

1 sq. = 1"

DONKEY

KING

SHEEP

KING

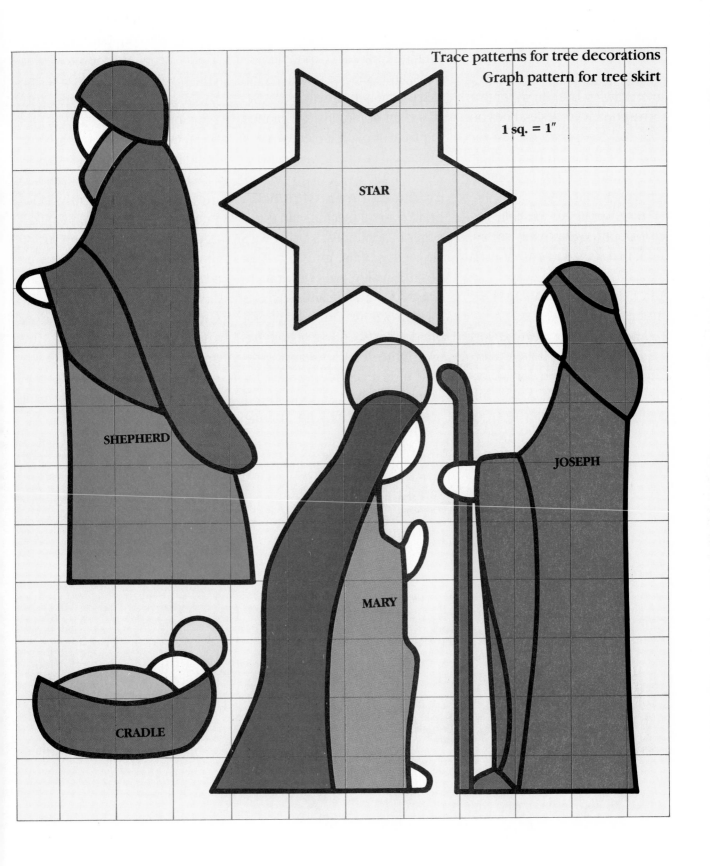

Trace patterns for tree decorations
Graph pattern for tree skirt

1 sq. = 1"

STAR

SHEPHERD

JOSEPH

MARY

CRADLE

**To Prepare Appliqués:** Enlarge patterns by copying on paper ruled in 1″ squares; transfer patterns to paper, one square at a time, drawing lines on paper that correspond with design lines on grid; make separate pattern for each appliqué, indicated by heavy outlines. Label and cut out patterns on outlines.

Trace appliqués on felt, following photograph for colors; mark five stars and one of each remaining appliqué shape. Cut out appliqués on marked outlines.

**To Appliqué:** Lay white tree skirt flat and arrange appliqués, referring to photograph for placement; pin in place. Assemble cradle pieces at center front of skirt opposite slit, butting appliqué edges. Assemble and arrange appliqués of people, animals, and stars, working around skirt on each side of cradle. When all appliqués are pinned in place, unpin felt pieces one at a time and carefully glue in place.

**To Attach Braid:** Glue black braid over all "seams" and outer edges of appliqués: Starting with shortest seams, glue braid in position, using it also to draw in or shape any details, such as Joseph's sleeve. Finish by gluing braid to cover outline of each figure. (**Note:** It is important to prevent glue from smearing right side of figures. Use glue gun if possible, or work with knitting needle to spread light coating of glue neatly on back of braid. Tight curves are the most difficult; it will help if you stick pins through braid and into felt, standing pins upright, as if they were on a pincushion, to hold braid in place until glue is set.)

When all appliqué edges are covered, cut and apply wool braid to inner and outer skirt edges in same manner, using pins to secure braid while glue sets; fold braid ends to wrong side of skirt at slit (skirt back). Glue red braid 1½″ from inner and outer skirt edges. Glue green braid in place 1″ inside red braid at outer skirt edge and ¾″ inside red braid at inner edge.

*Use the photograph as a guide for positioning the Nativity figures, beginning with the cradle and working outward on each side.*

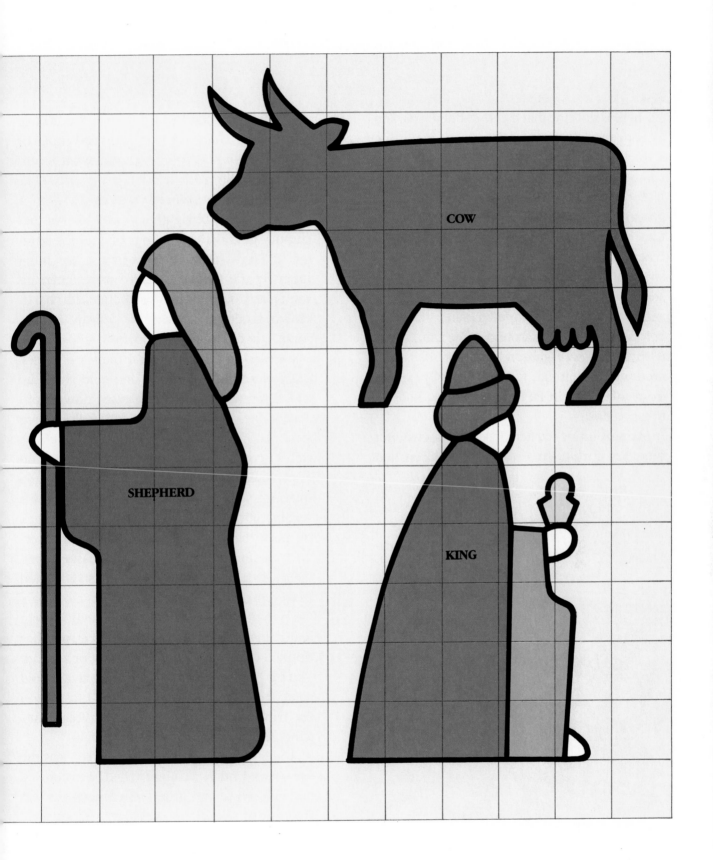

COW

SHEPHERD

KING

# The Tree

There is nothing that can so suddenly darken a room and fill it with enchantment as putting a thickly branched cedar in the corner. The room, even with its familiar furniture, the same pictures on the wall, was transformed into a grotto of incredible mystery. The tree perfumed the whole downstairs and anticipation reached a new peak. There has seldom been any project to match the way we dressed and adorned it. We hung it with strings of popcorn and cranberries. We looped garlands of multi-colored paper chains around it. We attached to its branches sweetgum and sycamore balls covered with tinfoil that we had carefully peeled from the paper in Pa Jim's Sir Walter Raleigh tobacco tins.

Mammy unlocked her closet, that sacrosanct reliquary forbidden to all her children and

grandchildren, and brought down the Box of Ornaments. There were age-softened ropes of tinsel, tarnished by time and somewhat moth-eaten from the yearly handling by excited children. There were colored pictures of angels on heavy paper and brightly colored turn-of-the-century girls with the wings of cherubs framing and crowding their portraits. We hung them on the tree first. There were glittering spun-glass balls, some of them with hand-blown indented sunsets or delicate spines, some tapered to points on both ends, some suspended within individual frames of tinsel. They were red and green and gold and blue and silver, and they were handed down from distant days when the family could afford such symbols of luxury. To us they were jewels, as rich in color as the accessories bedecking an imperious medieval queen but more fragile than egg shells. No matter that the color was scaling off or that there was a hole in the back of more than an occasional one. With reverence we unrolled them from their tissue paper, itself a little yellowed with age and so wrinkled from repeated use that it was soft as mole skin. Despite the care with which we handled them and hung them on the tree, their number thinned each year. A jostling elbow or an inadvertent brush against a suspending twig could send one of those gorgeous balls to crash upon the hardwood floor in shimmering fragments, a thousand tiny mirrors of our dismay.

The last ornament to go on the tree was the bird. Wondrously wrought, it had been colored red and white and green when new but was now mostly silver, its eyes worn smooth and sightless. Its little glass legs ended in points within balancing springs mounted on a rusted candle clip so that it swayed and trembled on the limb where we fastened it. It had the general configuration and noble proportions of a brown thrasher and was a Yuletide icon. Its long tail was made of the same kind of hair that was in our grandfather's shaving brush, and over the years that tail had become loosened. If the bird tilted the least bit forward, the entire tail disappeared into the body cavity so that the creature resembled a violated wren; consequently we were careful to perch him so that his head was raised to the ceiling as if triumphant in song and the splendid sweep of his tail was clearly visible. We learned early not to quarrel about who had the privilege of placing the bird on the tree. There was ample time to sneak alone into the room and change the position to suit oneself. Often that bird was moved a dozen times or more before Christmas Day, with never a voice raised in acrimony and with neither Baby Jesus dismayed nor Santa Claus one whit the wiser. The grownups said we were sweet while trimming the tree.

The foil icicles were last to go on. There was a flat cardboard box of them plucked from previous Christmas trees, but they were twisted and crumpled, their use requiring patience and care. Except in the very leanest years, our indulgent mother always bought two new packs folded straight in regimented rows. They were a delight to distribute, but we had to use the old ones first, to honor the gospel by Auntie and Mammy of "Waste not, want not." Sara and Janice and Jimmie draped the icicles one by one in rank and row on each individual limb. I was impatient and believed in tossing a hank of them toward the top of the tree and letting them fall in haphazard glitter where they might. I was usually excused from icicle duty; my sisters wanted that tree to be perfect. It always was.

We had no electric lights. In the daytime, light through the windows reflected from the balls and tinsel with the chilling wink of winter. Night was the real time of the tree. That was when it lived completely within the room. For the week before Christmas, we were allowed to build a fire in the parlor grate every night and at least knock the chill of refrigeration off the tall old room. The fire sheen brought the tree to life. Dressed in our footed pajamas with flaps in the seats, we watched the kaleidoscope of color dance through and over the somber mystery of cedar in such flicker and twinkle that we were bemused. The colors were richer because they were muted, and the mystery of Christmas filled our hearts. We understood little, but we sensed a great deal. When I was a little boy, every Christmas tree was perfect. Regardless of where the bird was perched.

*Ferrol Sams*

An excerpt from CHRISTMAS GIFT!

# *Jingle Bells*

Dashing through the snow
In a one-horse open sleigh,
O'er the fields we go
Laughing all the way;
Bells on bobtails ring,
Making spirits bright;
What fun it is to laugh and sing
A sleighing song tonight—Oh!

Jingle bells, jingle bells,
Jingle all the way!
Oh, what fun it is to ride
In a one-horse open sleigh!

*James Pierpont*

# Winter Warmers

*Handmade from the heart, colorful cozy outerwear keeps out winter's chill.*

# Red Warm-Up Set

## SIZE

Hat and mittens, medium. Scarf, 65″ long, plus fringe.

## EQUIPMENT

Knitting needles: For hat, set of dp needles Nos. 8 (5 mm) and 10½ (6½ mm). For scarf, knitting needles No. 10½ (6½ mm). For mittens, set of dp needles Nos. 8 (5 mm) and 10½ (6½ mm). Tapestry needle.

## MATERIALS

Reynolds Lopi, 100-gram skeins: For hat: 1 skein each red 103, white 51, and green 102. For scarf: 3 skeins red 103, 1 skein green 102, small amount of white 51. For mittens: 1 skein red 103, small amount of white 51 and green 102.

## GAUGE

10 sts = 3″ (No. 10½ needles).

## *Hat*

With red and No. 8 dp needles, cast on 70 sts. Divide sts on 3 needles. Join and work around in stockinette st (k each rnd) for 2″. Change to No. 10½ needles. Following Chart 1, repeat from A to B around. When top of tree is reached, cut green; work even for 3 rnds.

*First Dec Rnd:* * K 2 tog, k 5, k 2 tog, k 1 repeat from * around — 56 sts. K 4 rnds.

*Second Dec Rnd:* * K 1, k 2 tog, k 3, k 2 tog, repeat from * around — 42 sts. K 4 rnds.

*Third Dec Rnd:* * K 2 tog, k 1, repeat from * around — 28 sts. K 7 rnds. Cut yarn, leaving 10″ end. Pull through remaining sts, gather sts tog tightly and secure end.

**Embroidery**: With white, embroider snowflakes in duplicate st, following Chart 2. Embroider one line of snowflakes 3 rows apart directly over top of each tree, one line of snowflakes 3 rows apart between trees as shown. After each dec rnd, snowflakes will be 1 st closer tog.

**Finishing**: With white, make a 4″ pompon; see How-To's on page 75. Sew pompon to top of hat.

## *Scarf*

With red and No. 10½ needles, cast on 30 sts.

*Row 1* (right side): P 10, k 10, p 10.

*Row 2:* K 10, p 10, k 10. Repeat these 2 rows until piece is 65″ long. Bind off.

**Finishing**: Press scarf lightly, using thick damp cloth and warm iron. Holding bound-off edge toward you and following Chart 1, embroider tree in duplicate st on center knit panel of scarf near end. Cut green and white yarn into 10″ lengths. Holding 4 strands tog for each fringe, knot 5 green fringes on each side panel and 6 white fringes on center panel.

**CHART 1**

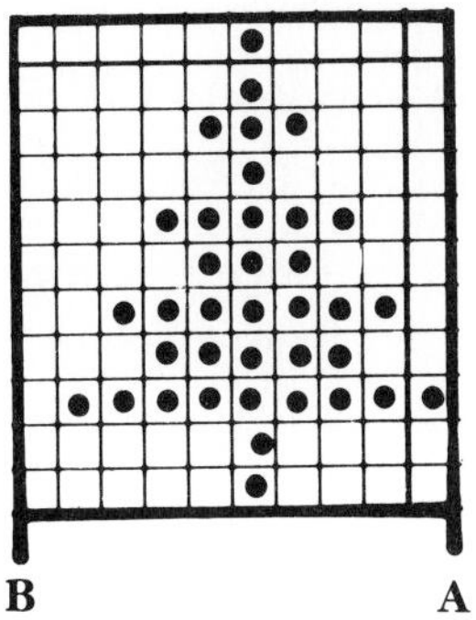

**Color Key**

- Green
- White

B          A

**CHART 2**

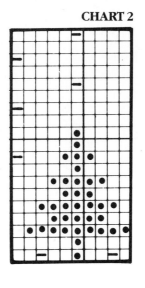

**CHART 3**

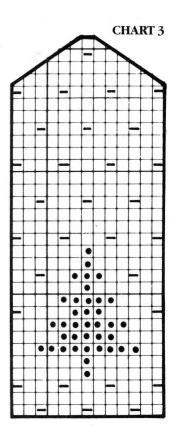

## Mittens

With red and No. 8 dp needles, cast on 24 sts. Divide sts on 3 needles. Join and work around in stockinette st (k each rnd) for 3½″. Change to No. 10½ needles. Work even for 3″.

*Thumb opening:* K 5, place these sts on a holder, finish rnd.

*Next Rnd:* Cast on 5 sts, finish rnd. Work even for 3¼″.

*First Dec Rnd:* * K 2 tog, k 2, repeat from * around. K 1 rnd.

*Second Dec Rnd:* * K 1, k 2 tog, repeat from * around. K 1 rnd.

*Third Dec Rnd:* * K 2 tog, repeat from * around. Cut yarn, leaving 10″ end. Pull through remaining 6 sts, gather sts tog tightly and secure end.

*Thumb:* Sl sts from holder to needle. Join yarn; k 4 of these sts to one needle; with 2nd needle, k 1, pick up and k 1 st at side of thumb and 2 sts on cast-on sts; with 3rd needle, pick up and k 3 sts on cast-on sts and 1 st at side of thumb—12 sts. Work even for 2″. K 2 tog around. Cut yarn, leaving 10″ end. Pull through remaining sts, gather sts tog tightly and secure end.

Work second mitten to correspond with first, reversing pattern and placement of thumb.

**Finishing:** Press mittens through thick damp cloth, having thumb at left of palm for left mitten and at right of palm for right mitten. Following Chart 3, embroider back of each mitten in duplicate stitch.

# Blue Warm-Up Set

## SIZE
Hat and mittens, medium. Scarf, 65″ long, plus fringe.

## EQUIPMENT
Knitting needles: For hat and mittens, set of dp needles No. 8 (5 mm) and 10½ (6½ mm). For scarf, knitting needles No. 10½ (6½ mm). Crochet hook size 1 (5½ mm). Tapestry needle.

## MATERIALS
Reynolds Lopi, 100-gram skeins: For hat and mittens: 1 skein each blue 98, green 102, and white 51. Few yards of yellow and red yarn. For scarf: 3 skeins blue 98; some green 102 and red 103, for fringe. Few yards of yellow yarn.

## GAUGE
10 sts = 3″ (No. 10½ needles).

### Hat
With blue and No. 8 dp needles, cast on 70 sts. Divide sts on 3 needles. Join and work around in stockinette st (k each rnd) for 2″. Cut blue. Change to No. 10½ needles. With yellow, work 1 rnd. Cut yellow. With white, work even for 2″. Join blue.

*Pattern: Rnd 1:* * With blue, k 1; with white, k 6, repeat from * around.

*Rnd 2:* * With blue, k 2; with white, k 4; with blue, k 1, repeat from * around.

*Rnd 3:* * With blue, k 3; with white, k 2; with blue, k 2, repeat from * around. Cut white. Work even with blue for 3 rnds.

*First Dec Rnd:* * K 2 tog, k 1, k 2 tog, k 5, repeat from * around —56 sts. K 1 rnd blue, 3 rnds white. Cut white and blue, join green.

*Second Dec Rnd:* * K 3, k 2 tog, k 1, k 2 tog, repeat from * around —42 sts. K 4 rnds green.

*Third Dec Rnd:* * K 2 tog, k 1, repeat from * around—28 sts. K 7 rnds green. Cut yarn, leaving 10″ end. Pull through remaining sts, gather sts tog tightly and secure end.

**Finishing:** With green, make 4″ pompon; see Making Pompons on page 75. Sew pompon to top of hat. With red, embroider a French knot at top of each white point.

### Mittens
With blue and No. 8 dp needles, cast on 24 sts. Divide sts on 3 needles. Join and work around in stockinette st (k each rnd) for 3½″. Change to No. 10½ needles. Work even for 3″.

*Thumb Opening:* K 5, place these sts on holder, finish rnd.

*Next Rnd:* Cast on 5 sts, finish rnd. Work even for 3¼″.

*First Dec Rnd:* * K 2 tog, k 2, repeat from * around, K 1 rnd.

*Second Dec Rnd:* * K 1, k 2 tog, repeat from * around. K 1 rnd.

*Third Dec Rnd:* * K 2 tog, repeat from * around. Cut yarn, leaving 10″ end. Pull through remaining 6 sts, gather sts tog tightly and secure end.

*Thumb:* Sl sts from holder to needle. Join yarn; k 4 of these sts to one needle; with 2nd needle, k 1, pick up and k 1 st at side of thumb and 2 sts on cast-on sts; with 3rd needle, pick up and k 3 sts on cast-on sts and 1 st at side of thumb—12 sts. Work even for 2″. K 2 tog around. Cut yarn, leaving 10″ end. Pull through remaining sts, gather sts tog tightly and secure end.

Work second mitten to correspond with first, reversing pattern and placement of thumb.

**Finishing:** Press mittens through thick damp cloth, having thumb at left of palm for left mitten and at right of palm for right mitten. Following chart, embroider snowman design in duplicate st on center back of each mitten. Sew small green pompon to top of snowman's hat. With blue, make 2 French knots for eyes. With yellow, embroider lazy daisy st nose. Cut 3 strands of red yarn 10″ long. Tie strands around snowman's neck, tying tog at center front. Braid each 3 ends; tie ends with white yarn.

### Scarf

With blue and No. 10½ needles, cast on 30 sts.

*Row 1* (right side): K 6, p 6, k 6, p 6, k 6.

*Row 2* (wrong side): P 6, K 6, p 6, k 6, p 6. Repeat these 2 rows until piece is 65″ long. Bind off.

**Finishing:** With yellow, work 1 row sc across each end of scarf. With blue, sc in each sc across.

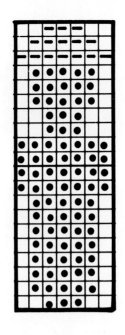

**Color Key**
- ▣ Green
- ▤ White

**STITCH DETAIL**

**Lazy Daisy Stitch**

**French Knot**

Steam-press scarf, using thick damp cloth and warm iron. Cut blue, green, and red yarn into 10″ lengths. Using 2 strands tog for each fringe, knot 5 fringes across center k 6 panel on each end of scarf. On one end, knot 5 red fringes, then 4 blue fringes on each side of center panel. On other end of scarf, knot 1 red, 4 green, and 4 blue fringes on each side of center panel.

## *Pretty Gauntlet Mittens*

### SIZE
Fits adult.

### EQUIPMENT
Crochet hooks sizes H (for mittens) and D (for "appliqués"). Tapestry needle.

### MATERIALS
Knitting worsted weight yarn: 2 oz. gray; green sport yarn; red sport yarn.

### GAUGE
4 sc = 1″; 5 rows = 1″.

### *Mitten directions*
(make 2): Ch 2 and, starting in 2nd ch from hook, ch 77.

*Row 1:* Sc in ch-11 to form front of cuff, sl st in ch-6 for wrist shaping, sc in ch-19 for hand, sl st in ch-4 for top of mitten, sc in ch-19 for back of hand, sl st in ch-6 for back of wrist, sc in ch-11 for back of cuff. Ch 1, turn.

For following rows, with exception of first and last sc in each row, work in *back lps* only. Rep Row 1 10 times.

*Thumb shaping:* Sc in sc-11 of cuff, sl st in 6-sc of wrist, sc in first 7-sc of hand, ch 13 for thumb.

Sk next 28 sc of hand, join to next sc, sc in last 7-sc of back of hand.

Sl st in 6-sc for wrist, sc in 11-sc of back of cuff. Ch 1, turn. Continue to work in *back lps.*

*First thumb row:* Sc in 11-sc of cuff, sl st in 6-sc of wrist, sc in first 7-sc of hand, sc in first 5 of ch for thumb. Sl st in ch-3 sps, sc in last 5 of ch for back of thumb. Sc in last 7-sc of back of hand, sl st in 6-sc for wrist, sc in 11 sc of back of cuff. Ch 1, turn. Repeat first thumb row 3 times. Fasten off after last rep.

**Finishing:** Fold mitten in half and, using tapestry needle and matching yarn, sew side seams with neat overcast stitch. Sew thumb seam. Make shamrock or strawberry appliqués.

## Shamrock Appliqué

Ch 2 and work 8 sc in first ch. Join with sl st and turn.

*To make first petal:* Ch 3, 4 dc in same sp. Turn.

*Rnd 1:* Ch 3 [first dc], dc in same sp, 1 dc in each of next 3 dc, 2 dc in last dc, ch 2, and turn.

*Rnd 2:* Dc in first st, hdc in next st, sl st in next 3 sts, dc, sc in last st. Break off yarn, leaving enough yarn to sew appliqué to mitten.

*To make second petal:* Sk 1 sc of first row and join yarn in next st. Work in same way as for first petal. Work 2 more petals in same way. Fasten off, leaving enough yarn to sew appliqué to mitten.

## Strawberry Appliqué

Using red yarn, ch 3, sc in last 2 chs, ch 1, turn.

*Row 1:* Inc 1 st each end, ch 1, turn. Work until there are 8 sc across row. Work even for 1 more row.

*Row 2:* Work sc in 3 sc, sl st in next 2 sc, sc in last 3 sc, ch 1, turn.

*Row 3:* Rep Row 2. Work 1 row sc around entire strawberry. End off.

*To make stem:* Join green yarn at top center of strawberry, ch 3, sk 2, 1 sc, ch 3, turn, sc in center. Ch 3, 1 sc in 2nd and 3rd ch, sc in center, ch 3, sk 2, 1 sc on other side of strawberry, ch 3, sc in center, ch 3. Fasten off.

**Finishing:** Using tapestry needle and matching yarn, secure the appliqué in position on back of mitten.

# No-Knit Holiday Sweater and Vest

*Put a young one in the holiday spirit — all decked out for Christmas in an easy-to-embroider Christmas tree sweater or appliquèd train vest.*

## Christmas Tree Sweater

### EQUIPMENT
Tapestry needle.

### MATERIALS
Purchased stockinette-stitch sweater. Scraps of yarn, same quality and thickness as sweater. Beads and sequins (optional).

### DIRECTIONS
Designs are worked by copying chart. Each square on chart represents one stitch on knitted fabric. Because knitted stitches are rectangular rather than square, design on knitted fabric will appear more flattened than it does on chart, so do not worry if your chart design seems to be slightly elongated and distorted.

Positioning of motifs and the number of repetitions is up to you. You may find that it helps to make small paper cutouts and pin these to garment, moving them around until you have a satisfactory arrangement.

Use each color separately, working as much as possible from right to left and then from left to right, to keep back of work neat and smooth. Keep an even tension while stitching, taking particular care not to pull yarn too tightly. Finish off ends at back of work by threading them through two or three stitches before cutting off excess yarn.

**Working the design:** Thread tapestry needle with yarn and begin at lower right-hand corner of motif to be worked. Secure end of yarn on back of work by running it under several stitches. Bring yarn through to front, through base of first stitch to be covered. Insert needle from right to left behind the stitch above.

Pull the yarn through. Insert needle through base of stitch and bring it out through base of next stitch to the left.

Pull yarn through, covering first stitch. Continue working in this manner across row, covering each stitch in turn and working from right to left. Work next row of stitches above first, working from left to right, as shown below.

For extra fun on Christmas day, you can sew colored beads and star-shaped sequins onto trees. If they make sweater look too specifically intended for Christmas, they can be taken off after holiday season.

**Duplicate Stitch Tree Motif**

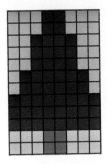

**Motif is 8 sts wide and 12 sts high.**

## *Train Vest*

### EQUIPMENT

Pencil. Ruler. Paper for patterns. Sharp scissors. Tapestry needle. Iron.

### MATERIALS

Purchased stockinette-stitch vest. (Vest should be pressable. If it is not, then sew appliqués to vest by hand, using embroidery floss or fine knitting yarn. Appliqués should be bonded only to smooth surface, such as stockinette stitch.) Small amount sport-weight yarn. Small amounts of washable, pre-shrunk, colorfast fabric for appliqués: red, yellow, green, and navy. Bonding fabric.

### DIRECTIONS

Following directions for Iron-On Appliqués, mark, bond, and cut out 1 engine, 2 cars, 1 window, and 6 each of inner and outer wheels. Arrange appliqués on vest front and back, following color photograph for placement; bond in place.

Using two strands sport-weight yarn in needle, embroider chain-stitch connectors between cars and engine; see Stitch Detail. Use white yarn to make three fairly flat pompons (see Making Pompons). Sew pompons to vest front as shown for "puffs" of smoke.

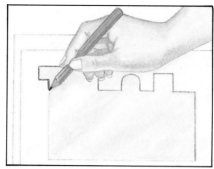

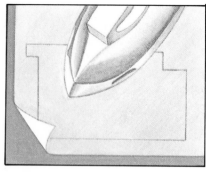

**IRON-ON APPLIQUÉS**
**1. Lay bonding fabric over pattern, paper side up. Trace pattern with pencil, remembering to reverse pattern when necessary.**

**2. With hot iron, press rough side of bonding fabric to wrong side of appliqué fabric until fibers stick firmly to fabric; see manufacturer's instructions.**

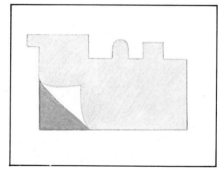

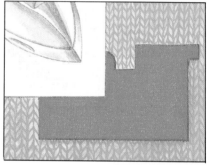

**3. Cut out shapes with sharp scissors, following pencil line carefully. Peel away paper backing from each appliqué.**

**4. Arrange shapes on knitting with wrong side of appliqué against right side of knitting. Cover with damp cloth; press. Let cool.**

**Chain Stitch**

## Making Pompons

For fuller, denser pompon increase size of central hole on cardboard templates so that more yarn can be wound around.

 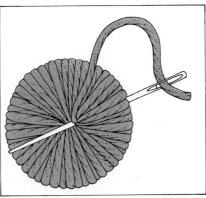 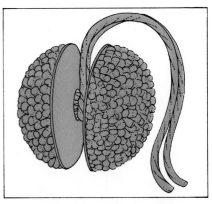

**1.** Cut two circles of thin cardboard desired size of finished pompon. Cut away a smaller circle from center of each piece.

**2.** Wind yarn evenly around both thicknesses of cardboard in the same direction until hole is filled. It may be easier to thread yarn through holes with a tapestry needle.

**3.** Cut yarn around outer edge, slipping blade of scissors between cardboard circles. Take a length of yarn and tie securely around center between the two circles. Remove cardboard, and fluff out pompon. Trim if desired.

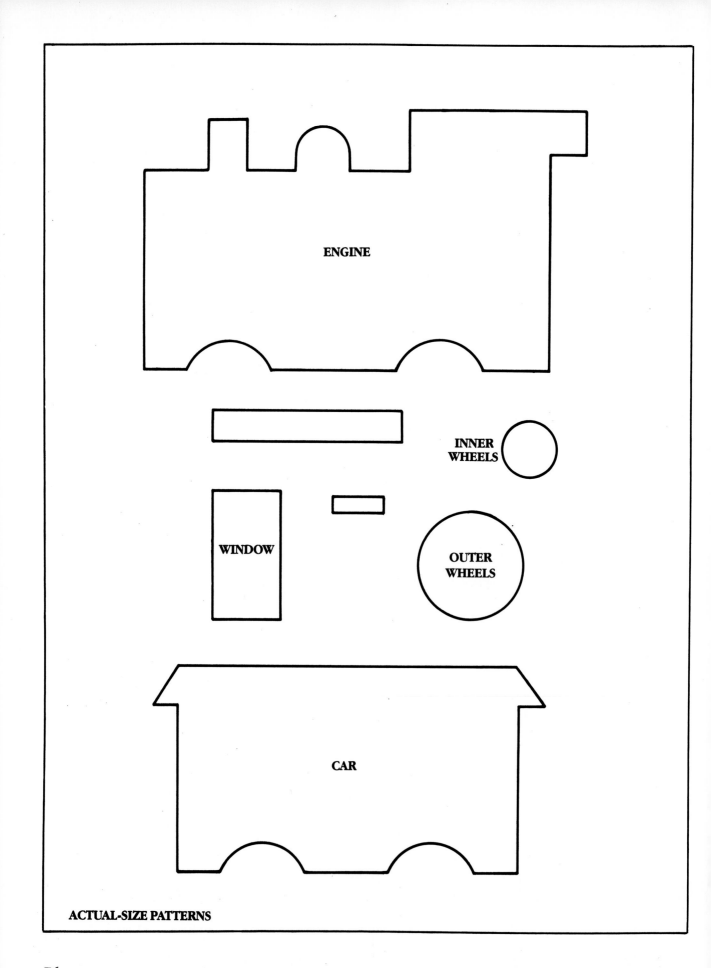

ENGINE

INNER
WHEELS

WINDOW

OUTER
WHEELS

CAR

**ACTUAL-SIZE PATTERNS**

# *Beyond Explanation*

They all were looking for a king
To slay their foes and lift them high:
Thou cam'st a little baby thing
That made a woman cry.

O son of man, to right my lot
Nought but thy presence can avail;
Yet on the road thy wheels are not,
Nor on the sea thy sail!

My fancied ways why shouldst thou heed?
Thou com'st down thine own secret stair;
Com'st down to answer all my need,
Yea, every bygone prayer!

*George MacDonald*

# Especially for Babies

*Festive holiday bibs let baby celebrate in style.*

**SIZES**
Small bibs, 10¼″ × 12¼″; large bib, 21″ long.

**EQUIPMENT**
Pencil. Ruler. Paper and thin, stiff cardboard for patterns. Glue. Scissors. Dressmaker's carbon paper. Dry ball-point pen. Straight pins. Sewing and embroidery needles. Sewing machine with zigzag attachment. Iron. Knitting needle.

**MATERIALS**
**For Noël Bib:** Two pieces white fabric 11″ × 13″, one terry cloth (or use hand towel), one cotton. White pre-gathered eyelet trim ¾″ wide, 1¼ yards. White double-fold wide bias tape, 1⅛ yards. Red and green sewing thread.

**For Christmas Ball Bib:** Two pieces cotton fabric 11″ × 13″, one white, one red. Fabric scraps: solid green, novelty print with Christmas motif about 4″ square (see color photograph). Batting. Light green sewing thread. Decorative print wide double-fold bias tape, 2¼ yards.

**For Holly Bib:** Two pieces cotton fabric 11″ × 13″, one red/green/ white striped, one white. Scraps of green and red cotton fabric. Batting. Red double-fold wide bias tape, 2¼ yards. Light green sewing thread.

**For Jack-in-the-Box Bib:** Terry cloth 45″ wide, ½ yard white (or use hand towel). White-dotted red cotton fabric 36″ wide, ½ yard (or 3½ yards wide double-fold bias tape and scrap of fabric to match). Small amount of red-dotted white fabric. Felt scraps: green, yellow, pale pink, white. Six-strand embroidery floss: blue, black, red. Scrap narrow red rickrack. One Velcro® tab. Fiberfill.

**For Each Bib:** Sewing thread to match fabric.

## GENERAL DIRECTIONS

Using ruler and pencil, draw lines across patterns, connecting grid lines. Enlarge each pattern by copying on paper ruled in 1″ squares; transfer pattern lines to paper, one square at a time, drawing lines on paper that correspond with design lines on grid. Heavy lines are pattern outlines. Make separate patterns for large and small bibs; do not complete half-patterns, indicated by long dash lines.

Following individual directions below, use dressmaker's carbon and dry ball-point pen to transfer each pattern to designated fabric or felt, placing long dash line of main bib pieces on fold of doubled fabric. Transfer machine-embroidery lines, indicated by short dash lines. Cut out appliqué pieces ¼″ outside marked outlines; cut out other pieces on lines. Make bibs as directed below; see Appliqué How-To.

**To Bind Raw Edges:** With right sides facing and raw edges even, pin one long edge of bias tape to raw edge of fabric; stitch in place along first fold line. Fold tape over, enclosing raw edges of fabric, and slip-stitch opposite folded edge to back of bib. Turn under short raw edges at ends; slip-stitch in place.

### Noël Bib

Read General Directions above. Use small bib pattern to cut front from white terry cloth and back from white cotton; transfer embroidery lines to right half of terry front only. Set sewing machine for close zigzag stitch. Using green thread for "Noël" and holly leaves, and red thread for berries, machine-embroider over dash lines, filling in holly. With right sides facing and raw edges even, pin eyelet trim around bib front, omitting neck edge; stitch in place. With right sides facing and eyelet trim in

between, stitch bib back to front, leaving neck edge open; turn bib to right side. With center of 40″ length of bias tape at center of neck edge, bind neck edge, following General Directions and leaving ends free for ties; slip-stitch long edges of ties closed.

### Christmas Ball Bib

Read General Directions above. Use small bib pattern to cut front from red cotton and back from white cotton. Also cut the following appliqué pieces: two green holly leaves and Christmas ball cut from novelty fabric, centering pattern over one motif (see color photograph). Use bib pattern to cut layer of batting same size. Sandwich batting between bib front and back; stitch in place all around, ¼″ from edge. Using light green thread, machine-appliqué ball and holly to bib front, following color photograph for placement. After all pieces have been appliquéd,

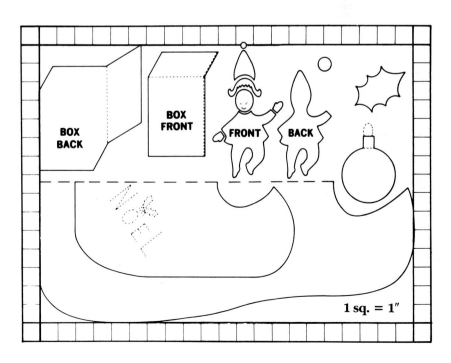

1 sq. = 1″

machine-embroider over dash lines, using close zigzag stitch for hanger and medium zigzag stitch for top of circle. Bind bib edges with decorative bias tape, binding neck edge separately and making ties as for Noël Bib.

### Holly Bib

Read General Directions above. Use small bib pattern to cut front from striped cotton (with stripes running vertically) and bib back from white cotton. Also cut the following appliqué pieces: two green leaves and three red berries. Use bib pattern to cut layer of batting same size. Sandwich batting between bib front and back; stitch in place all around, ¼″ from edge. Using light green thread for leaves and red thread for berries, machine-appliqué holly to bib front, following color photograph for placement. Bind bib edges with red bias tape, binding neck edge separately and making ties as for Noël bib above.

### Jack-in-the-Box Bib

Read General Directions above. Use large pattern to cut one bib (front) from white terry cloth. Cut the following appliqué pieces: box front from white-dotted fabric, box back from red-dotted fabric; reversing pattern, cut another box front from red-dotted fabric.

Cutting on the bias, cut 1¾″-wide strips of white-dotted fabric; piece as necessary to make strip 10′ long. Fold strip in half lengthwise; press. (**Note:** Purchased bias tape may be substituted.)

Using red thread, appliqué box back to bib, following color photograph for placement. Cut 12″ length of bias tape from prepared strip; stitch edges together. On box back, machine-embroider lid "crease" following dash line and catching one end of tape in "crease." With right sides facing and raw edges even, stitch two box fronts together along upper rim, making ⅛″ seam; turn to right side. Machine-embroider "corner" and upper rim, following dash lines. With red side up, appliqué box front over box back, matching bottom edges and leaving upper rim of box front free for opening.

Jack: Using patterns, cut one of each doll piece, following photograph for colors. Embroider face as follows, using two strands of floss in needle and referring to Stitch Details: two blue French-knot eyes; three black straight-stitch eyelashes above each eye; smiling mouth in red straight stitch. Assemble Jack as follows, using matching thread: Slip-stitch hair to top of head, leaving side "curls" free. Stitch bottom edge of face to body front at neck edge. Stitch rick-rack across body front as shown in photograph. Pin body front to body back with edges even and straight edges of hands sandwiched between arms; whip-stitch all around, leaving top of head open. Pin hat front to head back with edges even and "pom-pon" sandwiched between tips; stitch all around, leaving bottom

edge of hat open. Stuff Jack with fiberfill, using knitting needle to reach into arms and legs. Slip-stitch bottom of hat over top of hair. Cut 5″ length from prepared bias tape. With matching thread, baste a line lengthwise along center fold of tape; pull to gather to 2½″, forming "ruffle." Place ruffle around neck with basting thread at top and short raw edges meeting at back; stitch edges to back. Slip-stitch one half of Velcro® tab to center back of Jack; stitch opposite half to free end of tape extending from box. Bind bib edges with remaining bias tape, binding neck edges and making ties as for Noël Bib above.

## SPECIAL HINTS

Sheets of blue graph or quadrille paper can be purchased at art supply stores, and some sewing supply stores sell a special 1″ grid paper made for enlarging patterns.

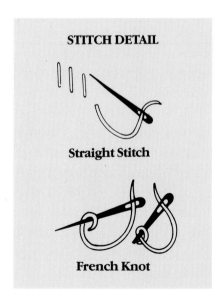

**STITCH DETAIL**

**Straight Stitch**

**French Knot**

## APPLIQUÉ

Choose a fabric that is closely woven and firm enough so a clean edge results when the pieces are cut. Press fabric smooth. There are two methods of transferring appliqué patterns to fabric:

**To Transfer Large Designs:** Mark a pattern on paper for each appliqué piece; do not cut out. Place paper on right side of fabric, inserting dressmaker's carbon paper between fabric and pattern. Go over lines of pattern with tracing wheel or dry ballpoint pen to transfer design. Remove pattern and carbon. Mark a second outline ¼" outside design outline. Appliqué as directed below.

**To Transfer Small Designs:** For each motif, make a cardboard pattern: Trace design; do not cut out. Glue tracing paper to cardboard and let dry; cut along traced line. Place cardboard pattern on right side of fabric. Holding sharp, hard pencil at an outward angle (light-colored pencil on dark fabric and dark pencil on light fabric), mark around pattern. When marking several pieces on the same fabric, leave at least ½" between pieces. Mark a second outline ¼" outside design outline. Appliqué as directed below.

**To Appliqué By Hand:** Using matching thread and small stitches, machine-stitch all around design outline, as shown in **Fig. 1**. This makes edge easier to turn and neater in appearance. Cut out appliqué on the outside line, as in **Fig. 2**. For a smooth edge, clip into seam allowance at curved edges and corners, then turn seam allowance to back, just inside stitching as shown in **Fig. 3**, and press. (**Note:** You may prefer to place some pieces so they overlap the extended seam allowance of adjacent pieces; study overall design before turning under all seam allowances.) Pin and baste the appliqués on the background — underneath pieces first — and slip-stitch in place with tiny stitches. See **Fig. 4**.

**To Appliqué By Machine:** Cut out appliqués on outside lines. Pin and baste appliqués in place; do not turn under excess fabric. Straight-stitch around appliqués on marked lines. Trim away excess fabric to ⅛" from straight stitching. Set sewing machine for close zigzag stitch as directed (¼" wide or less). Zigzag around appliqués, covering straight stitching and excess fabric.

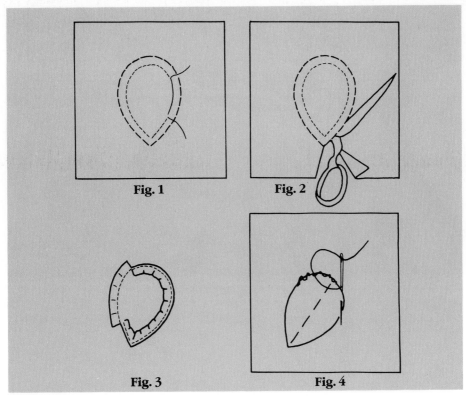

Fig. 1        Fig. 2

Fig. 3        Fig. 4

# *Partridge In a Pear Tree*

*A partridge in a pear tree heralds the onset
of the holiday season, contrasting a classic Christmas motif
and the bare elegance of silhouette stenciling.*

## SIZE
Finished card, 8″ × 6⅝″.

## EQUIPMENT
Pencil. Ruler. Tracing paper. Scissors. Crafts knife. White glue.

## MATERIALS
(for each card) Lightweight cardboard, piece 13¼″ × 8″ red or desired color. White posterboard, piece 6½″ × 5½″.

## DIRECTIONS
Trace design. Go over outline on wrong side of tracing; transfer it to posterboard, centering design so that there is a margin of at least ⅜″ all around white (outer) frame.

Carefully cut out design as shown in color photograph, making sure that enough paper remains to link areas, such as grass at side of picture and details on bird or fallen pears, where image changes from positive to negative.

Fold cardboard in half to make 8″ × 6⅝″ card with fold at top edge. For frame, cut out 5½″ × 4¾″ window centered on card front. To set white cutout behind open frame, put glue on back of frame, around edges, then position silhouette frame back and press in place.

### To Stencil
(optional): If you wish to make several cards, trace design and use carbon paper and dry ballpoint pen to transfer design to stencil board (available from art supply stores). Cut out design carefully and use to stencil directly on cardboard or on white posterboard, which can be framed in same manner as cutout silhouette. Use one or more colors, as desired.

# The Computer's First Christmas Card

jollymerry
    hollyberry
      jollyberry
        merryholly
          happyjolly
            jollyjelly
          jellybelly
        bellymerry
      hollyheppy
jollyMolly
    marryJerry
      merryHarry
        hoppyBarry
          heppyJarry

boppyheppy
berryjorry
jorryjolly
moppyjelly
Mollymerry
Jerryjolly
bellyboppy
jorryhoppy
hollymoppy
Barrymerry
Jarryhappy
happyboppy
boppyjolly
jollymerry
merrymerry
merrymerry
merryChris
ammerryasa
Chrismerry
asMERRYCHR
YSANTHEMUM

*Edwin Morgan*

85

# Cross-Stitch Cheer

*Delightful reindeer and bright red hearts spread Christmas cheer into the kitchen and onto the table.*

## Reindeer Pot Holders and Apron Set

### SIZE
Size of cross-stitch reindeer depends on mesh of waste canvas used.

### EQUIPMENT
Sewing needle. Embroidery needle. Scissors. Tweezers.

### MATERIALS
Apron and potholders suitable for cross-stitch. Waste needlepoint canvas. DMC embroidery floss. Sewing thread.

### DIRECTIONS
Baste waste canvas onto fabric, arranging it where reindeer is to be cross-stitched and securing it in place. Work cross-stitch with two strands floss in embroidery needle, following chart and working through both waste canvas and fabric at the same time. When stitching is complete, dampen waste canvas throughly; pull away threads of scrap canvas, using tweezers.

## Christmas Hearts Place Mats and Napkin Rings

### SIZES
Place mat, 16″ × 13″. Napkin ring, 2″ wide × 6″ around.

### EQUIPMENT
Ruler. Scissors. Straight pins. Sewing and embroidery needles.

### MATERIALS
Even-weave linen fabric #18, piece 20″ × 17″ for each place mat; 4″ × 8″ for each napkin ring. Sewing thread to match linen. DMC embroidery floss.

### DIRECTIONS
Neatly hem all fabric edges to make 16″ × 13″ placemat or 2″ × 6″ (flat) napkin ring. Using four strands floss in embroidery needle and following chart, cross-stitch large heart in corner(s) of mat; cross-stitch small heart in center of flat ring piece. Finish napkin ring by slip-stitching ends together at center back.

**Color Key**

Y  307   •  666

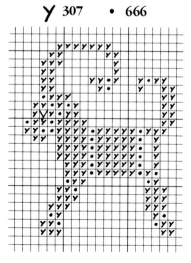

**Color Key**

⊿  Gold   •  666

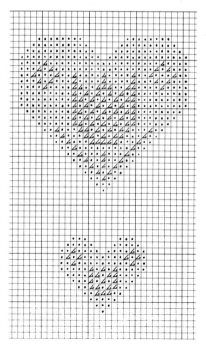

# Gumdrop Express

*This candy-studded choo-choo delivers holiday cheer for young and old with its cargo of sweet delights.*

## EQUIPMENT

Pencil. Ruler. Tracing paper. White cardboard (posterboard). White glue. Scissors. Sharp knife. Pastry bag with #3 tip. Soft, clean towel. Jars or cans, to be used as assembly supports.

## MATERIALS

Architectural Gingerbread Dough and Royal Gingerbread Icing (see recipes). Paste food coloring: red and yellow. Round lollipops about 2″ diameter with sticks cut off, 2. Round flat gumdrops, 16. Small candy canes, 4. Jelly beans. Gumdrops. Round red/white peppermint "pinwheels," 9. Assorted candies, for trims. Small juice can. Aluminum foil.

## Architectural Gingerbread Dough

- 1½ cups margarine *or* butter (3 sticks) *or* solid shortening
- 2¼ cups granulated *or* brown sugar
- 1½ tsp. salt
- 1½ tsp. baking soda
- 7 tsp. ground ginger
- 4 tsp. ground cinnamon
- 2 tsp. ground cloves
- 2 tsp. grated nutmeg (freshly grated, if possible)
- 1 tsp. ground cardamom
- 1½ cups molasses, dark *or* light
- ½ cup water
- 7-8 cups all-purpose flour (*not* self-rising)

In large mixing bowl, cream margarine and sugar; if using electric mixer, set it on low or medium speed, to avoid "fluffiness." Blend in salt, soda, and spices. Stir in molasses and water. Add 4 cups flour; mix thoroughly. Stir in remaining 4 cups flour, one cup at a time, until well-mixed. Wrap dough tightly in plastic. Chill or freeze for later use.

## Royal Gingerbread Icing

- 3 egg whites
- ½ tsp. cream of tartar
- 3½ cups (1 lb.) confectioners' sugar, sifted
- ½ tsp. orange *or* lemon extract (optional)

Mix all ingredients at low speed of electric mixer for 2 minutes, then 5-8 minutes on moderately high speed, or until it forms peaks with a spoon. If peaks do not form after maximum time, beat icing for a minute or two at a higher speed. Icing dries out quickly; keep it covered with a damp cloth or tightly fitting lid. It is best to make one batch at a time. It can be frozen to use later, but quality will diminish. Tint icing with paste food colors, using clean toothpick to transfer colors.

## DIRECTIONS

Trace and label actual-size patterns, using ruler to mark straight edges. Glue tracings to cardboard; let dry. Cut along marked outlines, for templates; do not cut out windows. Set templates aside.

Make dough and icing. Preheat oven to 350°. Lightly grease cookie sheets. On floured surface, roll out small amount of dough to ⅛″ thickness. Use template to cut out 6 stars: For each, lightly flour template and place on rolled-out dough; cut along template edges, using sharp knife. Smooth all cut edges with fingers.

Roll out remaining dough to ¼″ thickness. Cut out 7″ × 2¾″ rectangle for engine and roll out dough to ⅛″ thickness. Cut juice can to measure 2½″ long. Cover outside of can completely with foil; tuck ends to inside of can. Wrap dough rectangle around foil-covered can, centering can between dough ends; pinch dough seam together, to seal. Place can, seam side down, on cookie sheet; chill in freezer for 10 minutes. Use templates to cut remaining shapes from dough, referring to original patterns for number needed of each shape. Bake juice-can engine for about 12 minutes. Bake cut-out shapes for 10-20 minutes.

Decorate train pieces on flat surface, following color photograph: Pipe window outlines with white icing; fill in windows with yellow. Pipe lines between panels on cow catcher. Pipe borders and other trims as shown or as desired. For caboose, ice roof and sides; dip side edges in sprinkles; add peppermint candies and candy-cane smokestack. For each car, attach 2 flat gumdrops to each long side, for wheels.

Assemble each car flat on towel: Place one car side on towel, icing side down; attach base and ends with icing, supporting pieces with jars until icing is set. Turn car over and attach second side. Stand cars upright after all sides, ends, and bases are in place. Attach roof to engine and caboose. Ice engine roof and cover with jelly beans; add gumdrop smokestack and lollipop back wheels; attach cow catcher to engine front at a slight angle as shown. Add finishing touches as desired.

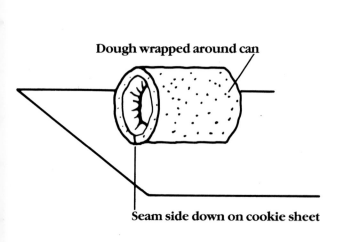

**Dough wrapped around can**

**Seam side down on cookie sheet**

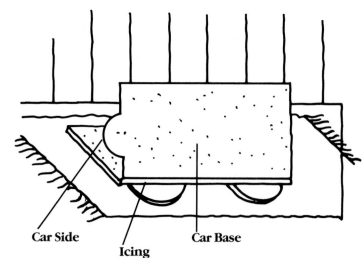

**Car Side**     **Icing**     **Car Base**

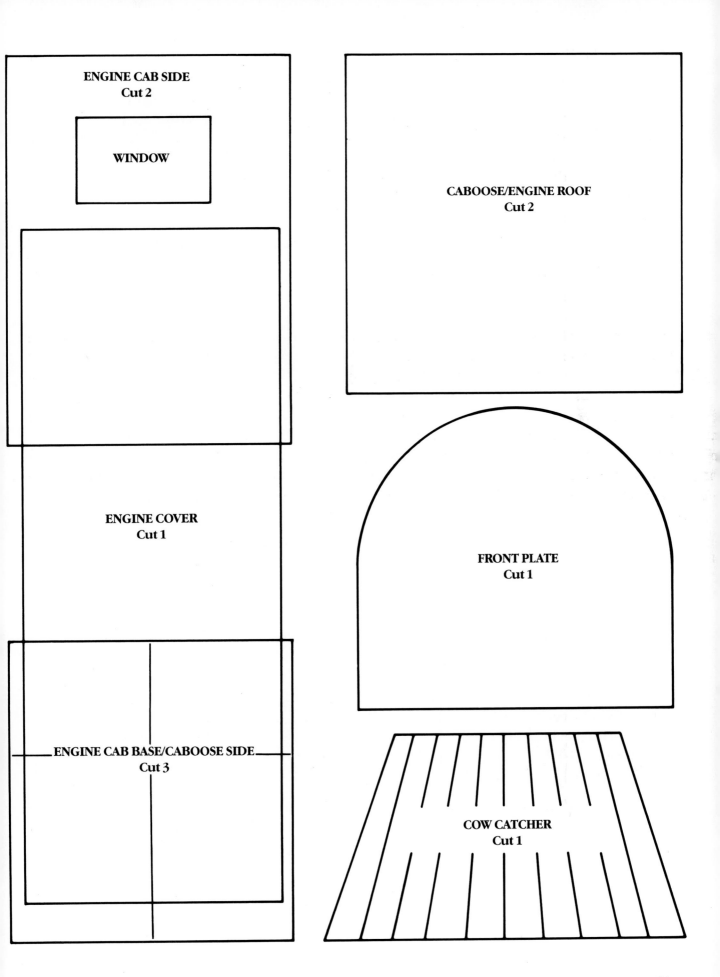

ENGINE CAB SIDE
Cut 2

WINDOW

ENGINE COVER
Cut 1

ENGINE CAB BASE/CABOOSE SIDE
Cut 3

CABOOSE/ENGINE ROOF
Cut 2

FRONT PLATE
Cut 1

COW CATCHER
Cut 1

91

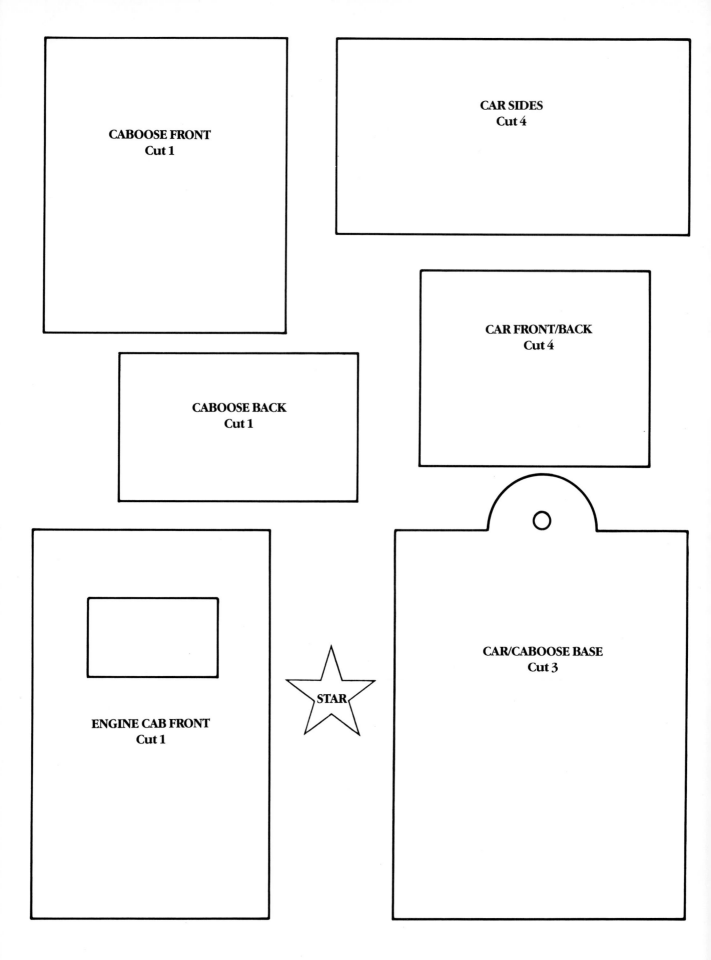

CABOOSE FRONT
Cut 1

CAR SIDES
Cut 4

CABOOSE BACK
Cut 1

CAR FRONT/BACK
Cut 4

CAR/CABOOSE BASE
Cut 3

ENGINE CAB FRONT
Cut 1

STAR

*Bringing Home the Tree*

# The Man Who Missed Christmas

It was Christmas Eve, and, as usual, George Mason was the last to leave the office. He walked over to a massive safe, spun the dials, swung the heavy door open. Making sure the door would not close behind him, he stepped inside.

A square of white cardboard was taped just above the topmost row of strongboxes. On the card a few words were written. George Mason stared at those words, remembering...

Exactly one year ago he had entered this selfsame vault. And then, behind his back, slowly, noiselessly, the ponderous door swung shut. He was trapped — entombed in the sudden and terrifying dark.

He hurled himself at the unyielding door, his hoarse cry sounding like an explosion. Through his mind flashed all the stories he had heard of men found suffocated in time-vaults. No time clock controlled this mechanism; the safe would remain locked until it was opened from the outside. Tomorrow morning.

Then the realization hit him. No one would come tomorrow — tomorrow was Christmas.

Once more he flung himself at the door, shouting wildly, until he sank on his knees exhausted. Silence came, high-pitched, singing silence that seemed deafening. More than thirty-six hours would pass before anyone came — thirty-six hours in a steel box three feet wide, eight feet long, seven feet high. Would the oxygen last? Perspiring and breathing heavily, he felt his way around the floor, he found a small, circular opening. Quickly he thrust his finger into it and felt, faint but unmistakable, a cool current of air.

The tension release was so sudden that he burst into tears. But at last he sat up. Surely he would not have to stay trapped for the full thirty-six hours. Somebody would miss him. But who? He was unmarried and lived alone. The maid who cleaned his apartment was just a servant; he had always treated her as such. He had been invited to spend Christmas Eve with his brother's family, but children got on his nerves, and expected presents.

A friend had asked him to go to a home for elderly people on Christmas Day and play the piano — George Mason was a good musician. But he had made some excuse or other; he had intended to sit at home with a good cigar, listening to some new recordings he was giving himself.

George Mason dug his nails into the palms of his hands until the pain balanced the misery in his mind. Nobody would come and let him out. Nobody, nobody...

Miserably the whole of Christmas Day went by, and the succeeding night.

On the morning after Christmas the head clerk came into the office at the usual time, opened the safe, then went on into his private office.

No one saw George Mason stagger out into the corridor, run to the water cooler, and drink great gulps of water. No one paid any attention to him as he left and took a taxi home.

There he shaved, changed his wrinkled clothes, ate breakfast and returned to his office, where his employees greeted him casually.

That day he met several acquaintances and talked to his own brother. Grimly, inexorably, the truth closed in on George Mason. He had vanished from human society during the great festival of brotherhood; no one had missed him at all.

Reluctantly, George Mason began to think about the true meaning of Christmas. Was it possible that he had been blind all these years with selfishness, indifference, pride? Wasn't giving, after all, the essence of Christmas because it marked the time God gave His own Son to the world?

All through the year that followed, with little hesitant deeds of kindness, with small, unnoticed acts of unselfishness, George Mason tried to prepare himself...

Now, once more, it was Christmas Eve.

Slowly he backed out of the safe, closed it. He touched its grim steel face lightly, almost affectionately, and left the office.

There he goes now in his black overcoat and hat, the same George Mason as a year ago. Or is it? He walks a few blocks, then flags a taxi, anxious not to be late. His nephews are expecting him to help them trim the tree. Afterwards, he is taking his brother and his sister-in-law to a Christmas play. Why is he so happy? Why does this jostling against others, laden as he is with bundles, exhilarate and delight him?

Perhaps the card has something to do with it, the card he taped inside his office safe last New Year's Day. On the card is written, in George Mason's own hand: *To love people, to be indispensable somewhere, that is the purpose of life. That is the secret of happiness.*

*J. Edgar Park*

# A Christmas Prayer

Loving Father,

    Help us remember the birth of Jesus, that we may share
in the song of the angels, the gladness of the shepherds,
and the worship of the wise men.

    Close the door of hate and open the door of love
all over the world.

    Let kindness come with every gift and good desires
with every greeting.

    Deliver us from evil by the blessing which Christ brings,
and teach us to be merry with clear hearts.

    May the Christmas morning make us happy to be
Thy children, and the Christmas evening brings us to our beds
with grateful thoughts, forgiving and forgiven,
for Jesus' sake. Amen!

*Robert Louis Stevenson*

# *Christmas Beside the Hearth*

# The Gift of Sharing

It was Christmas Eve, 1933. Mama was preparing to bake her "hardtimes fruitcake," so called because the only similarity to fruit it contained was prunes. But it was, to our family, an extra-special cake. My sisters, Lottie, Vivian, Estelle and Dolly, and I sat around our kitchen table, shelling pecans for the cake.

None of us, except Mama, was enthusiastic, and I suspected her gaiety was partly put on. "Mama," I asked, "why can't Grandma and Aunt Ella, and Aunt Fran and Uncle Hugh, and all the cousins come for Christmas like last year? We won't even have any music unless Joe comes and brings his guitar."

We wouldn't mind not having a Christmas tree because we'd never had one, and Mama and Daddy had prepared us for the possibility of no presents, but the thought of no visitors or music really subdued us. Dolly, age five and the youngest, sobbed.

"Why'd we have to move, anyway?" she asked, sniffling. So Mama again explained her version of Dust Bowl economics.

"When we had to give up our farm, we were lucky to find this place to rent, even if it is too far for the relatives to come. Don't worry, though," Mama reassured us. "Why, God might send us company for Christmas right out of the blue, if we believe strong enough." She began to pit the boiled prunes and mash them.

As we worked, a wind came up and whistled through the newpaper we'd stuffed into the cracks in the corners. A cold gust blasted us as Daddy entered through the back door after doing the chores at the barn. "It looks like we're in for a blue norther," he said, rubbing his hands together.

Later, Daddy built up a roaring cow chip and mesquite fire in the potbellied stove in the living room, and we were about to get into our flannel nightgowns when someone knocked on the door. A traveler, wrapped in his bedroll, had missed the main road and stopped to ask for shelter from the storm for the night.

"Mind you," he said, when he'd had a cup of hot coffee, "I don't take charity. I work for my keep. I'm headed for California. Heard there's work to be had there."

Then Mama fixed our visitor a cozy pallet behind the stove. We girls went into our bedroom and all crawled into the same bed for warmth. "Reckon he's the one Mama said God might send out of the blue for Jesus' birthday?" I whispered.

"He must be. Who else'd be out in weather like this?" Lottie said, and Vivian and Estelle agreed. We snuggled, pondered, and slept.

At breakfast our guest sopped biscuits in gravy. "I never had a family that I remember," he said. "Can't recollect any name 'cept Gibson. You can call me Mr. Gibson if you want." He smiled, revealing gums without teeth. Seemingly, he had no possessions beyond his bedroll and the clothes he wore, but he pulled a large harmonica from his pants pocket and said, "I've always had this. Want me to play something?"

So Mr. Gibson spent Christmas Day with us, and what a delight he was! He helped with the work, told us stories and played all the beloved Christmas songs on his harmonica. He played by ear as we sang church hymns. After much pleading on

our part, he agreed to stay one more night.

The next morning, when we awakened, Mr. Gibson was gone. I found his harmonica on the kitchen table. "Oh, Mama," I cried, "Mr. Gibson forgot his harmonica — the only thing he had."

Mama looked thoughtful. "No," she said softly. She picked it up and ran her palm over the curlicues etched in the metal sides. "I think he left it on purpose."

"Oh, I see," I said, "sort of a Christmas present. And we didn't give him anything."

"Yes, we did, honey. We gave him a family for Christmas," she said, and smiled.

We never saw Mr. Gibson again. Daddy had an ear for music and quickly learned to play the harmonica. Through the years, it brought many a joyful memory of that unforgettable Christmas when God sent us Mr. Gibson right out of the blue — a blue norther, that is — because He knew how much a man with music, who longed for a family, and a family without music, who longed for company, needed each other.

*Doris Crandall*

# Gift Foods

*Family, friends, and co-workers will get into the holiday spirit after receiving one of these special, homemade treats from your kitchen. Chocolate Pumpkin Truffles, Fruitful Cranberry Conserve, and a fresh, citrus fruitcake give new twists to old favorites.*

## Nut And Pumpkin Pound Cake

- 1¾ cups all-purpose flour
- ½ cup pecans, finely chopped or ground
- 1½ teaspoons ground cinnamon
- 1 teaspoon baking soda
- ½ teaspoon salt
- ½ teaspoon ground mace
- ¼ teaspoon ground nutmeg
- 1 cup butter, softened
- ¾ cup granulated sugar
- ½ cup light brown sugar (packed)
- 3 eggs
- 1 cup solid pack pumpkin
  Marzipan Bow (follows)

Heat oven to 325°. Grease and flour a 9×5 inch loaf pan. In medium bowl, combine flour, nuts, cinnamon, baking soda, salt, mace, and nutmeg; set aside. In large mixer bowl, cream butter and sugars. Add eggs; beat until light and fluffy. Mix in pumpkin and dry ingredients; beat well. Pour into loaf pan. Bake approximately 1 hour 15 minutes, or until wooden pick inserted in center comes out clean. Cool in pan 10 minutes; turn onto wire rack to cool completely.

**Makes 1 large loaf.**

### Marzipan Bow

- 1 package (7 ounces) marzipan or almond paste

Lightly dust board with confectioners' sugar. Roll out marzipan or almond paste into rectangle 4-inches wide, 20-inches long, and ¹⁄₁₆-inch thick. Cut into four ½-inch wide strips. Arrange two strips over loaf to create tied-package effect. Create ribbon bow ends by cutting two 5-inch lengths. Attach at point where marzipan ribbons cross; press to hold. Make bow by creating two ribbon loops; pinch center. Add bow where ribbons cross; press to hold.

## Holiday Fruitcakes

- 2 eggs, lightly beaten
- 1 can (30 ounces) pumpkin pie mix
- 2 packages (17 ounces each) date bread mix
- 3 cups candied cherries, halved
- 2 cups walnuts *or* pecans, coarsely chopped
- 1 cup prepared mincemeat
- 1 cup golden raisins

Heat oven to 325°. Grease generously mini bundt pans. In large bowl, beat eggs and pumpkin together. Blend in date bread mix. Stir in cherries, nuts, mincemeat, and raisins. Spoon into prepared pans, filling ¾ full. Bake 40 to 45 minutes, or until wooden pick inserted in center comes out clean. Cool in pans 10 minutes. Turn onto wire rack to cool completely.

**Makes 18 mini bundts.**

## Chocolate Pumpkin Truffles

- 2½ cups vanilla wafers, crushed
- 1 cup ground almonds, toasted
- ¾ cup confectioners' sugar, sifted
- 2 teaspoons ground cinnamon
- 1 cup (6 ounces) semisweet chocolate pieces, melted
- ½ cup solid pack pumpkin
- ⅓ cup coffee liqueur *or* apple juice

In medium bowl, combine crumbs, ground almonds, ½ cup confectioners' sugar, and cinnamon. Blend in melted chocolate, pumpkin, and liqueur. Form into 1-inch balls. Refrigerate. Dust with remaining confectioners' sugar just before serving.

**Makes 4 dozen truffles.**

## Holiday Almond Treats

- 2½ cups vanilla wafers, crushed
- 1¾ cups ground almonds, toasted
- ½ cup confectioners' sugar, sifted
- ½ teaspoon ground cinnamon
- 1 cup pumpkin pie mix
- ⅓ cup almond liqueur *or* apple juice

In medium bowl, blend crumbs, 1 cup ground almonds, confectioners' sugar, and cinnamon. Stir in pumpkin pie mix and liqueur. Form into 1-inch balls. Roll in remaining ¾ cup ground almonds. Refrigerate.

**Makes 4 dozen balls.**

## Autumn Jam

- 1 can (30 ounces) pumpkin pie mix
- ½ cup lemon juice
- 2 teaspoons ground ginger
- 1 package (1¾ ounces) dry fruit pectin
- 4½ cups granulated sugar

In large saucepan, combine pumpkin pie mix, lemon juice, ginger, and pectin. Heat to boiling, stirring constantly. Add sugar. Heat to rolling boil, stirring constantly. Continue boiling 1 minute, stirring frequently.

Skim off foam, if necessary. Pour into prepared jars.

**Makes 6 cups.**

### SAFETY TIP

When preparing and storing jam, follow manufacturer's instructions for sealing jars. Label and date.

## Golden Crown Honey Pound Cake

- 1 cup butter *or* margarine, room temperature
- ½ cup honey
- ½ cup granulated sugar
- 1 tablespoon vanilla extract
- 1 tablespoon grated lemon peel
- 3 eggs, room temperature
- 2 cups all-purpose flour
- 1 teaspoon baking powder
- ¼ teaspoon salt
- ¼ teaspoon baking soda
- 1 cup whole maraschino cherries, drained
- ½ cup broken pecans

Heat oven to 325°. Grease and flour three 6 × 3¼ × 2½ inch loaf pans. In large mixer bowl, beat butter on medium speed 1 minute. Gradually add honey and sugar. Beat 5 to 7 minutes. Add vanilla and lemon peel; mix well. Add eggs, one at a time, beating after each addition. Scrape bowl frequently. Combine flour, baking powder, salt, and baking soda; mix well. Add flour mixture to egg mixture; beat on low speed until ingredients are blended. Gently stir in cherries and pecans. Pour batter into pans. Bake 40 to 50 minutes, or until wooden pick inserted in center comes out clean. Cool 15 minutes. Remove from pan; cool

completely on wire rack.

**Makes 3 loaves.**

**Variation**: One 9 × 5 × 3-inch loaf pan may be used. Bake at 325° 1 hour.

## Honey Roasted Bridge Mix

- ½ cup honey
- 2 tablespoons butter *or* margarine
- 1 teaspoon ground cinnamon
- 4 cups mixed nuts (no peanuts)
- 2 to 3 tablespoons superfine sugar

Heat oven to 325°. Line a cookie sheet or jelly roll pan with foil. Combine honey, butter and ½ teaspoon cinnamon in saucepan. Bring to boil; boil and stir constantly 2 minutes. Pour honey mixture over nuts and toss until nuts are coated. Spread on prepared pan. Bake 10 to 15 minutes, or until nuts are glazed and lightly browned. *Do not allow nuts to burn.* Cool 20 to 30 minutes; remove from foil.

Combine sugar and remaining cinnamon; toss with glazed nuts to coat.

**Makes 4 cups.**

## Brandied Maraschino Cherries

3 jars (10 ounces each) maraschino cherries
1 pint brandy
¼ cup granulated sugar

Drain cherries; reserve 1 cup syrup. In a 2-quart jar, combine reserved syrup, brandy, and sugar; stir until sugar is completely dissolved. Stir in drained cherries. Store in tightly covered jar in cool place for 2 weeks.

**Makes about 5 cups.**

### SPECIAL HINTS
Serve over ice cream, or drain and use cherries for thumbprint cookies or other cookies. Remaining syrup may be served as a cordial.

### SAFETY TIP
When preparing and storing fruit, be sure to follow manufacturers instructions for sealing jars. Label and date.

## Glazed Colonial Cranberry Breads

4 cups unbleached all-purpose flour
1 cup granulated sugar
1 cup light brown sugar (packed)
2 teaspoons baking soda
2 teaspoons cream of tartar
1 teaspoon ground cinnamon
1 teaspoon ground allspice
½ teaspoon freshly grated nutmeg
½ teaspoon salt
Large pinch freshly ground black pepper
2 tablespoons grated orange zest (page 152)
1½ cups freshly squeezed orange juice (about 3 large oranges), remove seeds, but keep pulp
6 tablespoons unsalted butter, melted
2 eggs
4 cups fresh or frozen cranberries, rinsed and drained
1 cup pecans or walnuts

Heat oven to 350°. Place rack at center level. Butter and flour six small foil or aluminum loaf pans, 5¾ × 3¼ × 2 inches, or three 1-quart foil or aluminum loaf pans, 8 × 3¾ × 2½ inches or two 1½-quart loaf pans; set aside. In a large mixer bowl, sift together flour, sugars, baking soda, cream of tartar, cinnamon, allspice, nutmeg, and salt. Add black pepper and stir gently to blend. Spoon orange zest into food processor; set aside.

In medium mixer bowl or large measuring cup, whisk together orange juice, butter, and eggs until blended; set aside. Add cranberries and nuts to food processor; pulse several times, just until cranberries are coarsely chopped. *Do not overprocess.*

Make a "well" in dry ingredients; pour in liquid mixture and stir very lightly with large rubber spatula, just until mixture is slightly moistened. Add cranberry mixture and gently fold *just* until blended. Spoon batter into prepared pans, filling about ⅔ full. Tap each pan on work surface to remove air bubbles; gently smooth tops of batter.

Place filled pans on baking sheet, spacing them apart slightly, and place in oven. Bake 50 to 60 minutes, or until loaves are golden and a wooden pick inserted in the center comes out clean. *Do not overbake.* Turn loaves onto wire rack set over a large sheet of waxed paper. Carefully turn loaves right side up and cool. Prepare Nutmeg-Rum Glaze. With teaspoon, drizzle loaves with glaze, forming lines back and forth across narrow width of each loaf. Cool completely. Wrap each loaf in plastic wrap and return each to its foil pan.

**Makes 6 small loaves, or 2 or 3 larger loaves.**

### Nutmeg-Rum Glaze

2 cups confectioners' sugar, sifted
2 tablespoons milk
2 tablespoons dark rum, brandy, or apple cider
½ teaspoon vanilla extract
1 teaspoon fresh grated nutmeg

In small mixer bowl, stir together sifted confectioners' sugar, milk, rum, vanilla, and nutmeg. If necessary, add more rum or confectioners' sugar for a thin consistency to drizzle on loaves.

### SPECIAL HINTS
These loaves keep well, wrapped in plastic, for about 3 days. Freeze, tightly wrapped, if you'd like to store them longer.

## Grandma's Favorite Molasses Fruitcake

    2  oranges
    1  cup light molasses
    1  package (15 ounces) raisins
    1  package (8 ounces) dates, chopped
    2  containers (16 ounces each) glace fruit mix
    1  cup butter *or* margarine, softened
 1¼  cups granulated sugar
    6  eggs
    3  cups all-purpose flour
    1  teaspoon baking soda
 1½  teaspoons ground cinnamon
    1  teaspoon ground nutmeg
   ½  teaspoon ground allspice
   ½  teaspoon ground cloves
    1  cup orange juice, fresh squeezed
    2  cups nuts, halved

Heat oven to 300°. Grease a 10-inch bundt or tube pan. Cut oranges into large chunks. In blender or food processor, finely chop oranges. In large pot, combine chopped oranges, molasses, raisins, and dates; heat to boiling. Reduce heat; simmer 5 to 10 minutes. Remove from heat; stir in fruit mix; set aside. In large bowl, cream together butter and sugar. Beat in eggs, one at a time. Sift together flour, baking soda, and spices. Add to creamed mixture alternately with orange juice. Stir batter into molasses-fruit mixture. Add nuts. Spoon 8 cups batter into pan. With remaining 6 cups batter, make 2 dozen cupcakes *or* 8 dozen mini fruitcakes (see below). Bake 2 hours, or until wooden pick inserted in center comes out clean. Cool 10 minutes. Remove from pan; cool on wire rack. To

## Cranberry-Apricot Tea Cakes

 1¼  cups boiling water
   ¾  cup dried apricots
   ½  cup butter, softened
   ¾  cup granulated sugar
    2  eggs
 1½  teaspoons vanilla extract
 1¾  cups all-purpose flour
    2  teaspoons baking powder
   ½  teaspoon baking soda
   ½  teaspoon salt
    1  cup fresh *or* frozen cranberries, thawed and coarsly chopped
   ½  cup nuts, chopped
       Confectioner's sugar
       Cranberries (for garnish)

Heat oven to 375°. Grease and flour 2½-inch muffin cups, or line with paper liners. Pour boiling water over apricots. Allow to soak 15 minutes to soften. Drain; reserve ¾ cup of the liquid.

Cream butter with sugar until light and fluffy. Beat in eggs, one at a time, until well blended; beat in vanilla. Sift flour, baking powder, baking soda, and salt together. On low speed, add flour mixture in three additions, alternating with ¾ cup apricot liquid. Stir in cranberries, apricots, and nuts. Spoon batter into prepared muffin cups, filling each about ¾ full.

Bake 20 to 23 minutes, or until cakes are golden brown and a wooden pick inserted in center comes out clean. Let cool in pans 5 minutes. If you have not used paper liners, run a sharp knife around each cake to release. Turn onto wire rack to cool completely. Sift confectioners' sugar over tops of cakes before serving. Garnish each with a cranberry, if desired.

**Makes 22 tea cakes.**

serve, sprinkle with confectioners' sugar. Garnish with orange pieces and candied cherries, if desired.

### Variations

*"Cupcake" Fruitcakes:* Using 6 cups batter, spoon about ¼ cup batter into each of 24 paper-lined muffin cups (2½ × 1¼ inch). Press a candied cherry or nut half into top of each, if desired. Bake at 300° 40 to 45 minutes. Makes 2 dozen cup-cake-size fruitcakes.

*"Mini" Fruitcakes:* Using 6 cups batter, spoon about 1 tablespoon batter into each of 96 paper-lined "miniature" muffin cups (1¾ × 1 inch). Press a candied cherry or nut half into top of each, if desired. Bake at 300° 30 to 35 minutes. Makes 8 dozen miniature fruitcakes.

## Orange Cranberry Cake

- 1 can (8¼ ounces) crushed pineapple
- 2 cups all-purpose flour
- 1 cup granulated sugar
- 1 teaspoon baking soda
- ½ teaspoon salt
- 1 cup dates, chopped
- 1 cup almonds, chopped
- 2 eggs
- 1 cup whole berry cranberry sauce
- ¾ cup vegetable oil
- 1 tablespoon grated orange peel

Heat oven to 350°. Grease two 8½ × 4½ inch loaf pans. Drain pineapple. Combine flour, sugar, baking soda, and salt. Stir in dates and almonds. Combine

pineapple with eggs, cranberry sauce, oil, and orange peel; stir into dry mixture. Pour into loaf pans. Bake 1 hour. Cool in pans on wire rack 15 minutes.

Makes 2 loaves.

## Fruitful Cranberry Conserve

- 1 package (12 ounces) fresh *or* frozen cranberries, thawed
- 1 pound dried apricots, chopped
- 1½ pounds dried figs, chopped
- 1 package (15 ounces) golden raisins
- 1 lemon, chopped
- 1 orange, chopped

- 4 cups granulated sugar
- 6 cups water
- 1 teaspoon ground cinnamon
- 1 can (4 ounces) slivered blanched almonds

In a large saucepan or Dutch oven, combine all ingredients. Simmer 20 to 25 minutes, stirring occasionally to prevent sticking. While hot, spoon into sterilized jars. Seal and cool. Store in a cool, dry place.

Makes 4½ quarts.

### SAFETY TIP

When preparing and storing fruit, be sure to follow manufacturer's instructions for sealing jars. Label and date.

# Festive Bouillabaisse Dinner

*This steaming seafood stew makes a delicious informal dinner — the perfect dish to serve your guests at a tree-trimming party or before a night of caroling. Make the rice pudding and its sauces in advance for a light and festive finale.*

## Bouillabaisse

⅓ cup light olive oil
4 large cloves garlic, finely chopped
2 large onions, finely chopped
4 ounces fennel bulb, finely chopped
½ cup parsley sprigs, chopped
3 large pear-shaped tomatoes, chopped
1 tablespoon basil, finely chopped (1 teaspoon dried)
1 tablespoon fresh thyme leaves (1 teaspoon dried)
1 bay leaf
1/16 teaspoon saffron
Orange peel strip (1 × 3 inches)
1½ pounds littleneck clams, scrubbed
1½ pounds mussels, scrubbed
2 pounds fish fillets of choice
1 pound large shrimp, cleaned
3 quarts hot water
Chopped parsley, for garnish

Heat oil in a 5-6 quart pot over medium heat. Add chopped vegetables. Add basil, thyme, bay leaf, saffron, and orange peel. Cover; simmer vegetables 20 minutes. Add water and season to taste.

Heat ingredients to boiling. Reduce heat; simmer. Add clams in shells as well as any fish portions an inch or more in thickness. Cover pot. Cook about 8 minutes. Add mussels in shells. Cover; simmer. Cook 2 minutes. Add thin fish portions and shrimp; simmer. Cover and cook 3 to 4 minutes.

Remove fish and seafood to a warm platter. Taste broth and correct seasoning if necessary. Discard bay leaf and orange peel. Serve broth in bowls and garnish with chopped parsley. Pass fish on platter, allowing guests to choose fish and seafood they wish to add to broth.

**Makes 6 to 8 servings.**

## Spinach Cheese Loaf

2 eggs, lightly beaten
1 cup crumbled feta cheese
1 package (10 ounces) frozen chopped spinach, thawed, well-drained, and squeezed dry
1 teaspoon oregano leaves
1 clove garlic, minced
3 to 3½ cups all-purpose flour
1 package active dry *or* rapidrise yeast
1 tablespoon granulated sugar
1 teaspoon salt
1 cup water
1 tablespoon butter *or* margarine
1 egg white, lightly beaten
Sesame seed (optional)

In medium bowl, combine eggs, feta cheese, spinach, oregano, and garlic; set aside.

In large bowl, combine 1 cup flour, undissolved yeast, sugar, and salt. Heat water and butter until hot to touch (120° to 130°). Gradually add to dry ingredients; beat 2 minutes at medium speed, scraping bowl occasionally. Add ½ cup flour; beat 2 minutes at high speed, scraping bowl occasionally. With spoon, stir in enough flour to form soft dough. Turn dough onto lightly floured board; knead until smooth and elastic, about 5 minutes.

Roll dough to 14 × 10 inches. Place on greased baking sheet. Spread filling down center third of dough length. Make cuts from filling to dough edges at 1-inch intervals along each side of filling. Alternating sides, fold strips, at an angle across filling. Cover; let rise in warm, draft-free place 15 minutes.

Brush with egg white; sprinkle with sesame seed, if desired. Bake at 400° 25 minutes, or until done. Cool slightly. Serve warm.

**Makes 1 loaf.**

## *Seasoned Bread Ring*

- 4 to 4½ cups all-purpose flour
- 3 tablespoons granulated sugar
- 2 packages active dry *or* rapidrise yeast
- 1½ teaspoons Italian herb seasoning
- 1 teaspoon salt
- ¾ cup milk
- ¼ cup water
- ¼ cup plus 3 tablespoons butter *or* margarine
- 1 egg, room temperature
- ¼ cup poppy seed *or* Aromatic Seed & Pepper Mix (follows)

In large bowl, combine 1½ cups flour, sugar, undissolved yeast, herb seasoning, and salt. Heat milk, water, and ¼ cup butter until hot to touch (120° to 130°F). Gradually add to dry ingredients; beat 2 minutes at medium speed, scraping bowl occasionally. Add egg and ½ cup flour; beat 2 minutes at high speed, scraping bowl occasionally. With spoon, stir in enough flour to form soft dough. Turn dough onto lightly floured board; knead until smooth and elastic, about 7 to 8 minutes. Cover; let rise 20 minutes for active dry yeast; 10 minutes for rapidrise yeast.

Melt remaining butter. Grease 10-inch tube pan with small amount of melted butter. If pan has removable bottom, line with foil before buttering. Sprinkle 1 tablespoon poppy seed in bottom of pan.

Punch down dough; divide into 30 pieces. Roll each to smooth ball. Dip 15 balls in melted butter and arrange in bottom of pan. Sprinkle with 1½ tablespoons poppy seed. Dip remaining balls in butter and place in pan, making 2 layers. Drizzle remaining butter over rolls and sprinkle with remaining seed. Cover tightly with greased plastic wrap; refrigerate for 2 to 24 hours.

Remove from refrigerator, uncover dough and let stand 10 minutes. Bake at 375° for 35 minutes (25 minutes for dark or nonstick-coated pans). Cover with aluminum foil to prevent excess browning. Bake additional 10 minutes, or until done. Cool in pan on rack 20 minutes. Invert onto plate to serve.

**Makes 1 loaf.**

### Aromatic Seed & Pepper Mix
Roll balls in combination of 1 teaspoon cracked black pepper mix with poppy, sesame, caraway, celery, and/or cumin seed to measure ¼ cup.

### *SPECIAL HINTS*
*To bake immediately:* Cover; let rise in warm, draft-free place until doubled in size, about 30 minutes. Bake as directed.

## Rice Pudding with Raspberry Sauce and Crème Anglaise

1⅓ cups cooked rice
1⅓ cups milk, scalded
¼ cup granulated sugar
⅛ teaspoon salt
2 eggs, beaten
1 teaspoon vanilla extract
Raspberry Sauce (follows)
Crème Anglaise (follows)
Whipped cream for garnish (optional)
Fresh raspberries for garnish (optional)

Heat oven to 350°. Grease 8 molds. Combine rice, milk, sugar, and salt; whisk in eggs and vanilla. Pour rice mixture into molds. Place molds in pan filled halfway up side with hot water. Bake 30 to 35 minutes, or until knife inserted in center comes out clean. Cool.

To serve, pour equal amounts of Raspberry Sauce and Crème Anglaise on individual serving plates. Unmold pudding on serving plates. Garnish each serving with whipped cream and fresh raspberries, if desired.

Makes 8 servings.

### Raspberry Sauce

1 package (10 ounces) frozen sweetened raspberries, thawed
2 teaspoon cornstarch

Combine raspberries (with syrup) and cornstarch in small saucepan over medium heat. Heat, stirring constantly, 5 to 7 minutes, or until thickened. Strain mixture; cool.

### Crème Anglaise

1 cup milk
2 tablespoons granulated sugar
2 teaspoons cornstarch
1 egg yolk, beaten

Combine milk, sugar, and cornstarch in small saucepan over medium heat. Heat, stirring constantly, 5 to 7 minutes, or until almost thickened. Whisk 2 tablespoons of hot mixture into egg yolk; stir back into hot mixture. Heat, stirring constantly, 1 to 3 minutes. Cool.

# Sincerely...

It is late Christmas Eve. The fire has burned to embers, the children are asleep. My husband is assembling a doll stroller. I hand him a screwdriver and as I lean back on the carpet my eyes light on a tiny blue and silver rocking horse on the Christmas tree. The ornament is a remnant of my childhood. And as I stare at it, memories wander out of the past...

I am a child and it is nearly Christmas. I stand on a kitchen chair pummeling cookie dough with a rolling pin. I wallop the bag of flour right off the counter and it explodes in a cloud of white dust. I do not move, waiting for Mama to explode too. But she doesn't. "What's your favorite cookie shape?" she asks calmly. I find my voice. "A star." Smiling, she hands me the tin cutter. "Make lots of stars while I clean up," she says.

My daddy lifts me onto the seat of his old farm truck and carries me deep into the cold woods to find a Christmas tree. I tramp by a dozen or more that he points out. On and on. I finally choose one, and he says, "Yes, ma'am, I believe this was worth waiting for." He chops it down, loads it onto his big shoulders, and holds my hand all the way back to the truck.

I am sitting in the darkness of my childhood home, gazing at the little tree...at a blue and silver rocking horse near the top. Mama calls me to the window and points out a star, big and Bethlehem-bright. We lean on the sill and remember the holy night in a silence that is deeper and richer than any words I have ever heard...

The door in time closes as quietly as it opened and I'm an adult again, staring at the ornament and thinking how precious memories are. They live in our hearts and minds, waiting to whisper back to us. Sometimes they come in difficult times, giving strength and hope. Or they come simply to touch us with affection.

Now all at once it occurs to me that perhaps those memories most likely to whisper back do not fall happenstance into our lives. Instead they are *created.* They are handmade by those who have the imagination — and patience to turn bits and pieces of time into something beautiful for others. It doesn't take much. A pan of cookie stars in a warm kitchen. Holding hands in the woods.

Sandy has finished the doll stroller; a new doll is tucked inside. Silence, now, beside the tree. Then the rustle of a small nightgown at the door. "Oh, Mama!" cries Ann, spying the stroller through the sleep in her eyes. She hugs the doll. I blink at her. Now what? She has spoiled the surprise. But above us the blue and silver horse glistens.

"Want to carry your new doll to bed?" I ask suddenly.

She nods. They will wake up on Christmas morning already friends. But more special still, perhaps on a Christmas Eve yet to come, she too will remember...

*Sue Monk Kidd*

# A Kiss Of Chocolate

*Indulge in the magical spirit of Christmas! For chocolate lovers of all ages these sumptuous cookies are a festive, tasty treat.*

## Chocolate Chip Fruit and Nut Bars

- ½ cup butter *or* margarine, softened
- ¾ cup brown sugar (packed)
- 1 egg
- ½ teaspoon vanilla extract
- 1¼ cups all-purpose flour
- ½ teaspoon baking soda
- ½ teaspoon salt
- 1 cup mixed candied fruit (cut up apricots, raisins, red and green cherries)
- ¾ cup semisweet chocolate pieces
- ½ cup nuts, coarsley chopped
  Filling (follows)

Heat oven to 350°. Grease baking pan, 13 × 9 × 2 inches. Cream butter, sugar, egg, and vanilla until smooth. Combine flour, baking soda, and salt; blend into creamed mixture. Spread evenly in pan. Bake 12 to 15 minutes or until lightly browned. Cool.

Prepare Filling. Spread evenly over crust. Sprinkle candied fruits, chocolate pieces, and chopped nuts evenly over filling. Bake 15 minutes. Cool completely. Cut into bars.

**Makes about 36 bars.**

### Filling

- 2 tablespoons granulated sugar
- 2 tablespoons milk
- 1 tablespoon butter, melted
- ½ teaspoon vanilla extract
- 1 egg
- ⅓ cup all-purpose flour
- ½ teaspoon baking soda
- ¼ teaspoon salt

In small mixer bowl, combine sugar, milk, butter, vanilla, and egg until smooth. Add remaining ingredients. Beat until well blended.

## Peanut Butter Glazed Chocolate Bars

- ¾ cup butter *or* margarine
- ½ cup unsweetened cocoa
- 1½ cups granulated sugar
- 1½ teaspoons vanilla extract
- 3 eggs
- 1¼ cups all-purpose flour
- ¼ teaspoon baking powder
  Peanut Butter Filling and Glaze (follows)
  Chocolate Drizzle (optional; follows)

Heat oven to 350°. Line a 15½ × 10½ × 1 inch jelly roll pan with aluminum foil. Grease foil; set aside. Melt butter in medium saucepan over low heat. Add cocoa; stir constantly until smooth. Remove from heat; stir in sugar and vanilla. Beat in eggs, one at a time, until well blended. Stir in flour and baking powder. Spread evenly in pan. Bake 14 to 16 minutes, or until top springs back when lightly touched in center. Remove from oven; cool 2 minutes. Invert onto cooling rack. Peel off foil; turn right-side-up on rack to cool.

Prepare Peanut Butter Filling and Glaze. Cut in half crosswise; spread half of glaze evenly on one half. Top with second half; spread with remaining glaze. Cool to set.

Prepare Chocolate Drizzle. Drizzle over peanut butter glaze; if desired. After chocolate is set, cut into bars.

**Makes about 40 2 × 1 inch bars.**

### Peanut Butter Filling and Glaze

- ¼ cup granulated sugar
- ¼ cup water
- 1 cup peanut butter pieces

In small saucepan, combine sugar and water; bring to boil. Remove from heat. Immediately add peanut butter pieces. Stir until melted. Cool slightly.

**Makes about 1 cup glaze.**

### Chocolate Drizzle

- ⅓ cup semisweet chocolate pieces
- 1 teaspoon shortening

Melt semisweet chocolate pieces with shortening in top of double boiler over hot, *not boiling*, water. Stir until melted.

# Chocolate Cherry Cookies

⅔ cup butter *or* margarine
¾ cup granulated sugar
1 egg
1½ teaspoons vanilla extract
1⅔ cups all-purpose flour
6 tablespoons unsweetened cocoa
¼ teaspoon baking powder
¼ teaspoon baking soda
⅛ teaspoon salt
18 maraschino cherries, well-drained and halved
Chocolate Glaze (follows)

Heat oven to 350°. Cream butter, sugar, egg, and vanilla until fluffy. Stir together flour, cocoa, baking powder, baking soda, and salt; add to creamed mixture. (Dough will be stiff.) Shape into 1-inch balls. Place 1 inch apart on ungreased baking sheets. Place a cherry half on top of each cookie. Bake 8 to 10 minutes, or until no imprint remains when touched with finger. Cool on wire rack.

Prepare Chocolate Glaze. Frost each cookie, leaving top of cherry showing.

**Makes about 3 dozen cookies.**

## Chocolate Glaze

2 tablespoons granulated sugar
2 tablespoons water
½ cup semisweet chocolate pieces

In small saucepan, combine sugar and water. Cook over medium heat, stirring constantly, until mixture boils and sugar is dissolved. Remove from heat; *immediately* add chocolate pieces. Stir until melted. Cool until glaze is of spreading consistency.

# Mocha-Frosted Drops

1½ cups all-purpose flour
½ teaspoon baking powder
½ teaspoon baking soda
¼ teaspoon salt
½ cup shortening
2 squares (2 ounces) unsweetened chocolate
1 cup brown sugar (packed)
1 egg
½ cup buttermilk *or* sour milk
1 teaspoon vanilla extract
1 package (6 ounces) semisweet chocolate pieces
½ cup walnuts, chopped
Mocha-Butter Frosting (follows)

Heat oven to 350°. Combine flour, baking powder, baking soda, and salt; set aside. In saucepan, melt shortening and unsweetened chocolate over low heat. Remove to large mixer bowl; cool 10 minutes. Stir in brown sugar. Add egg, buttermilk, and vanilla; beat until smooth. Add dry ingredients to egg mixture; beat well. Stir in chocolate pieces and walnuts. Drop from teaspoon 2 inches apart onto greased cookie sheet. Bake 10 minutes. Cool 1 minute. Remove to wire rack; cool completely. Prepare Mocha-Butter Frosting; frost drops.

**Makes about 42 drops.**

## Mocha-Butter Frosting

¼ cup butter *or* margarine
2 tablespoons unsweetened cocoa
2 teaspoons instant coffee
2½ cups confectioners' sugar, sifted
1¼ teaspoons vanilla extract
2 to 3 tablespoons milk

Blend together all ingredients, adding enough milk to make frosting of a creamy spreading consistency.

# Butter-Nut Chocolate Topped Cookies

½ cup butter *or* margarine
½ cup granulated sugar
1 egg
1 teaspoon vanilla extract
1¼ cups all-purpose flour
¼ teaspoon baking soda
⅛ teaspoon salt
30 foil-wrapped milk chocolate pieces
½ cup almonds, pecans, *or* walnuts, finely ground

Heat oven to 350°. In small mixer bowl, cream butter, sugar, egg, and vanilla until well blended. Combine flour, baking soda, and salt; add to creamed mixture, beating well. Form dough into 1-inch balls. (If dough is soft, chill until firm enough to shape.)

Meanwhile, unwrap milk chocolate pieces. Roll balls in ground nuts; place on ungreased cookie sheet. Bake 10 to 12 minutes, or until almost no imprint remains when lightly touched in center. Remove from oven. Immediately press a milk chocolate piece into center of each cookie. Carefully remove cookies from sheet; cool on wire rack. Chill, if necessary, to set chocolate before storing.

**Makes about 2½ dozen cookies.**

**Variation:** Add ¾ teaspoon grated orange rind to creamed mixture.

## *Hazelnut Chip Sandies*

- 1   cup butter *or* margarine
- ⅓   cup granulated sugar
- 2   teaspoons vanilla extract
- 2   teaspoons water
- 2   cups all-purpose flour
- 1   package (6 ounces) miniature semisweet chocolate pieces
- ½   cup chopped hazelnuts (filberts)
- ¼   cup confectioners' sugar, sifted
- 1   tablespoon shortening Chopped hazelnuts (filberts)

Heat oven to 325°. In a mixer bowl, beat butter on medium speed for 30 seconds. Add granulated sugar; beat until fluffy. Add vanilla and 2 teaspoons water; beat well. Stir in flour, ½ cup chocolate pieces, and ½ cup chopped hazelnuts. Shape dough into 1½ × ½ × ½-inch crescents. Place on ungreased cookie sheet.

Bake 25 minutes, or until edges are firm; cool. In a plastic bag gently shake a few cookies at a time in confectioners' sugar.

In a small saucepan, melt remaining chocolate pieces and shortening; carefully dip one end of each cookie into the chocolate mixture. Sprinkle chocolate lightly with chopped hazelnuts. Place cookies on a cookie sheet lined with waxed paper; chill until set.

**Makes about 36 cookies.**

# Christmas Bells

I heard the bells on Christmas Day
Their old, familiar carols play,
And wild and sweet
The words repeat
Of peace on earth, good-will to men!

*Henry Wadsworth Longfellow*

# Traditional English Christmas Dinner

*Roast beef with "all the trimmings" is an English custom we're proud to continue, particularly when the trimmings include fresh-from-the-oven Yorkshire Popovers. Very often, tiny prizes were hidden in the traditional "figgy" pudding served for dessert. Our Amaretto Fig Cake is an updated version that's definitely a prize in itself.*

## Christmas Standing Rib Roast

4  to 6 pound beef standing rib roast
1  cup beef broth *or* water
   Yorkshire Popovers (follows)

Heat oven to 325°. Place roast, fat side up, in open shallow roasting pan. Do not add water. Do not cover. Insert meat thermometer so tip is centered in the thickest part of meat. Roast until meat thermometer registers 135° for rare, 155° for medium, and 165° for well done. Allow 26 to 32 minutes per pound for rare, 34 to 38 minutes per pound for medium, and 40 to 42 minutes per pound for well done. Roasts continue to cook after removal from the oven. Therefore, let "set" for 15 minutes before carving. Drain excess grease from roasting pan. Leave beef drippings and reserve 3 tablespoons grease for Yorkshire Popovers. Place pan on stovetop over high heat. Add beef broth; cook and stir until broth is reduced to about ¾ cup and brown bits are dissolved. Strain into gravy boat and serve with roast and Yorkshire Popovers.

**Makes 8 to 12 servings.**

### SPECIAL HINTS

For a 6 to 8 pound roast, allow 23 to 25 minutes per pound for rare, 27 to 30 minutes per pound for medium, and 32 to 35 minutes per pound for well done.

Potatoes may be roasted around beef. After meat cooks 1 hour, place 2 pounds small red potatoes in roasting pan around beef; stir to coat with drippings. Cook until beef is done.

## Yorkshire Popovers

2  eggs
½  teaspoon salt
1  cup cold milk
1  cup flour

After removing roast from oven, increase heat to 400°. Brush twelve muffin or popover cups with some of the grease from the roasting pan. Heat muffin pans while preparing popover batter, about 5 minutes. Beat eggs until foamy; beat in salt and milk. Gradually stir in flour; beat until smooth. Divide batter among hot muffin cups. Immediately place in oven. Bake 30 minutes, or until puffed and dark golden. Serve immediately.

**Makes 12 popovers.**

## Elegant Berry Trifle

- 3 packages (3 ounces each) vanilla pudding and pie filling
- 1½ teaspoons almond extract
- ½ cup white grape juice
- ½ cup red raspberry fruit spread
- ½ cup blackberry fruit spread
- 1 loaf (12 ounce) pound cake, cut into ½-inch thick pieces
- 8 crisp almond macaroon cookies, crushed
- ¼ cup toasted slivered almonds Whipped cream

Prepare pudding mix according to package directions; cool. Blend in 1 teaspoon almond extract. Combine remaining extract with grape juice; set aside.

Evenly distribute red raspberry spread on ¼ of pound cake slices; repeat procedure with blackberry fruit spread on ¼ of cake slices. Top each jam-spread cake slice with plain cake slice to form "sandwiches". Cut each "sandwich" into ¾-inch wide pieces; reserve a few to garnish top of trifle. Sprinkle remaining cake pieces with grape juice mixture.

To assemble trifle, spoon ⅓ of pudding into 6-cup dessert dish or trifle bowl. Alternate raspberry and blackberry cake pieces in pattern on pudding, using half of the pieces; repeat procedure. Top with layer of pudding. Chill several hours.

Shortly before serving, sprinkle top of trifle with crushed macaroon or slivered almonds along edge of dish; garnish with whipped cream and reserved cake pieces.

**Makes 6 servings.**

## Fig Amaretto Cake

- Butter
- ½ cup sliced almonds
- ⅔ cup butter
- 1 cup brown sugar (packed)
- 4 eggs
- ⅔ cup orange marmalade
- ⅓ cup dairy sour cream
- 2⅓ cups all-purpose flour
- 1¼ teaspoons baking soda
- ¼ teaspoon salt
- ⅔ cup almond liqueur
- 1 cup dried figs, snipped
  Confectioners' sugar

Heat oven to 350° Generously butter an 8½ inch (9 cup) bundt pan. Sprinkle with almonds, patting to adhere. Cream butter until light. Gradually add brown sugar and beat until fluffy. Beat in eggs, one at a time. Stir in marmalade and sour cream. (Mixture will look curdled.) Stir together flour, baking soda, and salt. Add flour mixture alternately with liqueur, beating after each addition. Stir in figs. Turn into cake pan. Bake 60 to 70 minutes, or until wooden pick inserted in center comes out clean. Cool in pan 10 minutes. Turn onto wire rack to cool completely. Dust with confectioners' sugar before serving.

**Makes 8 to 12 servings.**

# Christmas Turkey Dinner

*Like to try something new, but your family loves the traditional favorites? Citrus fruits add a fresh zest to this Christmas dinner. Enjoy Tangerine Stuffing, Orange Carrot Puff, and scrumptious Orange Holiday Cake.*

## Roast Turkey with Tangerine Stuffing

**10-12 pound turkey, fresh or frozen**
**Tangerine Stuffing (follows)**
**Gravy (follows)**

Follow directions on package for thawing frozen turkey. Wash turkey and pat dry. Remove neck and giblets. Rub cavity lightly with salt. (Do not salt if turkey is to be stuffed.)

Cook giblets in 4 cups water to make stock for gravy; reserve. Stuff turkey with Tangarine Stuffing and fasten with skewers.

Heat oven to 325°. Place turkey, breast side up, on rack in open shallow roasting pan. Brush with oil, butter, or shortening. Insert meat thermometer into breast or thickest part of thigh muscle. Roast until thermometer registers 185°. Cover drumsticks and breast with foil or cheesecloth when it starts to brown.

When turkey is done, remove and allow to stand about 20 minutes. Remove stuffing as soon as possible.

**Makes 10 to 12 servings.**

## Tangerine Stuffing

- 4 slices bacon
- ⅔ cup scallions, sliced
- ⅔ cup celery, chopped
- 6 cups fresh bread cubes (12 slices)
- 1¼ teaspoons grated tangerine rind
- 2 cups tangerine sections, pitted, cut in thirds (3 tangerines)
- ¼ cup parsley, chopped
- ½ cup chicken broth
- ½ teaspoon ground sage
- ½ teaspoon dried leaf thyme, crumbled
- ½ teaspoon salt
- Dash pepper

In medium skillet, cook bacon until crisp. Remove from pan, drain, and crumble. Using same skillet, sauté scallions and celery in bacon fat until soft. Add remaining ingredients; mix well.

**Makes about 6 cups (enough to stuff a 10 to 12 pound turkey).**

## Gravy

- 8 tablespoons all-purpose flour
- Drippings
- 2 cups reserved stock
- 4 chicken bouillon cubes
- ⅛ teaspoon pepper

Blend flour with drippings from turkey in roasting pan to form paste. Add stock, bouillon, and pepper. Blend in remaining stock. Cook over low heat until thickened, stirring constantly until thoroughly heated.

**Makes 4 cups.**

## Spiced Oranges

- 4 oranges, unpeeled
- 1 cup granulated sugar
- 1 cup honey
- ½ cup cider vinegar
- ¼ cup water
- 6 whole cloves
- 2 two-inch cinnamon sticks

Cut each orange into 8 wedges; remove seeds. Place oranges in large saucepan; add water to cover. Cover; simmer 30 minutes. Drain; discard water and rinse oranges well. Return to pan. Add sugar, honey, vinegar, ¼ cup water, cloves, and cinnamon.

Simmer 1 hour, uncovered. Skins should be tender and slightly transparent. Cool and serve, or pack slices in sterilized jars; fill with hot syrup, seal.

**Makes 1 quart.**

### SAFETY TIP

When preparing and storing fruit, be sure to follow manufacturer's instructions for sealing jars. Label and date.

## Orange Carrot Puff

2 pounds carrots
1 cup orange juice
3 eggs, separated
¼ cup all-purpose flour
¼ cup butter *or* margarine
   melted
2 tablespoons honey
¾ teaspoon grated orange rind
¾ teaspoon ground cinnamon
¾ teaspoon ground cardamom
½ teaspoon salt

Heat oven to 350°. Butter a 2½-quart casserole. Pare carrots; trim tops. Cut into 1-inch pieces. In a large skillet, cook, covered, in a small amount of boiling, salted water, 15 to 20 minutes, or until tender; drain. Combine carrots and orange juice in blender. Blend at high speed until carrots are puréed. Alternate ⅓ carrots and orange juice; repeat process with remaining carrots and juice.

In large mixer bowl, combine puréed carrots with lightly beaten egg yolks, flour, butter, honey, orange rind, cinnamon, cardamom, and salt; mix well. Beat egg whites until stiff, but not dry. Fold into carrot mixture. Pour into prepared casserole. Bake 45 minutes. Serve immediately.

**Makes 8 servings.**

## Orange Holiday Cake

6 eggs, separated
¾ cup granulated sugar
2 teaspoons grated orange rind
3 tablespoons orange juice
¼ teaspoon salt
1 cup cake flour, sifted
   Orange Sauce (follows)
   Orange Frosting (follows)
   Chocolate Curls

Heat oven to 325°. Butter and flour three 8-inch round cake pans. In large mixer bowl, beat egg yolks. Add sugar, orange rind, orange juice, and salt. Beat until light and fluffy, 5 minutes. Gradually stir in cake flour. Beat egg whites until stiff, but not dry; fold into egg mixture. Pour into prepared pans. Bake 30 minutes, or until cake springs back when gently pressed with fingertip.

Invert pans on wire rack to cool completely. Remove from pans. Pierce layers with a food pick. Gradually pour Orange Sauce over layers until all sauce is absorbed. Spread each layer with Orange Frosting. Assemble layers; frost sides of cake. Garnish with Chocolate Curls, if desired.

**Makes 10 to 12 servings.**

## Orange Sauce

¾ cup granulated sugar
¾ cup water
1 orange, sliced, with skin
¼ cup Marsala wine

In small saucepan, combine sugar and water. Bring to boiling. Stir to dissolve sugar; add orange slices. Simmer gently 15 minutes, or until liquid measures ⅔ cup. Remove from heat. Remove orange slices; add Marsala wine. Cool.

## Orange Frosting

2 eggs, beaten
⅔ cup granulated sugar
½ cup orange juice
¼ cup all-purpose flour
1 cup heavy cream, whipped

Combine eggs, sugar, orange juice, and flour in top of double boiler; mix well. Heat over boiling water, stirring constantly, until thick and smooth. Chill. Fold in whipped cream.

# Casual Holiday Party

*Your holiday guests might be reluctant to "ruin" this whimsical Christmas tree spread, but it's too good not to eat. Serve with zesty Tomato Ginger Punch, chicken bits, and dip for a complete party menu.*

### Christmas Tree Cheese Spread

1 envelope onion recipe soup mix
1 cup butter *or* margarine, softened
2 tablespoons milk
2 tablespoons prepared mustard
2 cups shredded Cheddar cheese (about 8 ounces)
2 cups shredded Swiss cheese (about 8 ounces)
2 tablespoons pimiento, chopped
Chopped parsley

In medium bowl, blend onion soup mix, butter, milk, and mustard; stir in cheeses and pimiento. Spoon onto serving platter, building up mixture to form the shape of a cone. Garnish by pressing parsley and, if desired, additional chopped pimiento onto cone; chill. Serve at room temperature.

**Makes about 5½ cups.**

## Easy Chicken Peanut Dip

- ¾ cup mayonnaise
- 1½ cups cooked chicken or turkey, finely chopped
- 1 cup celery, finely chopped
- 2 tablespoons onion, chopped
- 2 tablespoons lemon juice
- ½ cup roasted peanuts, chopped
- ¼ teaspoon pepper
  Chopped pimiento for garnish

In medium bowl, stir together all ingredients except pimiento. Cover; refrigerate until serving time, at least 2 hours.

Garnish with chopped pimiento and additional peanuts, if desired. Serve with crackers or fresh vegetables for dipping.

**Makes 3 cups.**

## Tomato Ginger Punch

- 3 cups vegetable juice
- 2 tablespoons lemon juice
- ½ teaspoon grated fresh ginger
- 1 bottle (12 ounces) sparkling apple juice
  Lemon slices for garnish

In medium pitcher, stir together vegetable juice, lemon juice, and ginger. Add apple juice.

To serve, pour over ice cubes in 10-ounce glasses. Garnish with lemon slices.

**Makes 4 servings.**

## Spicy Vegetable Punch

- 1 cup vegetable juice *or* no salt added vegetable juice
- 1 cup tomato juice
- 1 cup apple juice
- 1 cup cranberry juice
- 1 cup grapefruit juice
- 1 cup lemonade
- 1 cup orange juice
- 1 cup pineapple juice
- 8 drops hot pepper sauce

In large pitcher, stir together all ingredients. To serve, pour over ice cubes in 10-ounce glasses.

**Makes 8 servings.**

## Crunchy Chicken Bits

- ¼ cup cornstarch
- ½ teaspoon granulated sugar
- ¼ teaspoon onion powder
- ⅛ teaspoon garlic powder
- 2 tablespoons water
- 2 egg whites, lightly beaten
- 2 whole chicken breasts, skinned, boned, and cut into strips
- 2 cups cocktail peanuts, finely chopped
- 2½ cups peanut oil

In small bowl, stir together cornstarch, sugar, onion, and garlic. Stir in water. In small bowl, lightly fold cornstarch mixture into beaten egg whites. Dip chicken pieces into egg mixture to coat; roll in peanuts.

In deep-fat fryer or 4-quart saucepan, heat oil to 375°. Add 8 to 10 chicken pieces at a time. Cook until golden brown. Remove to paper towels to drain. Repeat with remaining chicken pieces. Serve hot as appetizers.

**Makes about 30 pieces.**

# The Philippines Without Chimneys

My mother tells this tale better than I do. It's really her story. But it remains one of the fondest Christmas memories of my life, and it illustrates to what strange lengths parents will go to keep the spirit of Christmas alive for their children.

I was seven. We lived in Manila. The Philippines is festive almost all year round anyway, but during Christmas the islanders catapult themselves into a frenzy of dancing and decorating. From every porch and balcony hang *parol* star lanterns. Creche scenes proliferate. Strings of flowers, foil, and candy drape the trees. The place goes crazy with lights and firecrackers.

We were living, like most Americans in Manila in the fifties, in pretty serious opulence. Our house was part of a walled-in cluster of homes that were scattered throughout the suburbs. The walls were topped with broken glass embedded in cement. It took us kids a while to figure out how to climb over them. In the front of the compound was a big iron gate and a Filipino guard with a gun.

Anyway, one of the purest expressions of the Christmas celebration swept through our compound that year. All these wonderful parties went on, with dancing in the garden, caroling, Christmas lights festooning the mango trees, candles and hibiscus blossoms floating in the pool, and chickens running loose with ribbons around their necks.

My little brothers and I were amazed by it all. The real magic was still to come, though — Santa Claus. We knew all about him, but we were getting old enough that we worried over details. How could Santa land his sleigh on our roof? We didn't have a chimney through which he could come down. No one had chimneys. Would he make it?

The kids in the compound talked about him and someone said there really wasn't a Santa Claus; he actually was your parents. Then someone else said there was so a Santa and you could prove it by leaving food out for him in the morning. If the food was gone, you had your proof.

I went to my mom and asked her if we could leave a sandwich and a glass of Coke out for Santa so he could have a snack. He would be hungry zooming all around the world delivering presents. His reindeer needed a snack, too — a big rice basket filled with grass. So we made Santa a bologna sandwich, poured the Coke, and my brothers and I pulled long grass from the edges of the lawn and put it in the rice basket. We put the sandwich and Coke by a tree in the yard and the basket outside on the porch.

Then we went to bed. Mom and Dad tucked us in, went downstairs, had a Christmas drink or two, ate all put part of the crust of the sandwich and poured out the flat Coke. Then they went to bed.

At three o'clock in the morning my mother woke up with a start. She thought, "My God, the reindeer's grass!"

She got up and went downstairs, out to the porch, grabbed the basket of grass and walked into the driveway. Where could she dump this stuff? Her boys played everywhere. They would certainly find it in the compound.

Our house was the third one in from the iron gate. The best place to dump the grass would be in the street outside the gate. So my mother went to the gate. She pulled the bolt. Just then the guard came out of the bushes with his rifle pointed right at her.

"Merry Christmas!" my mom said.

"Oh! Mrs. Goldsberry! Oh! Merry Christmas, mum."

"I just need to go outside for a second," my mom said.

The guard looked at her as if she were crazy, but put down his rifle and opened the gate. He watched her walk to the middle of the street and fling the grass out of the basket.

When she came back through the gate he said "Everything okay, mum?"

"Yes, thank you," she said. "Merry Christmas. *Maligayang Pasko.*" How could she explain what she had just done? She didn't even try.

"*Maligayang Pasko,*" the guard said.

My mother walked back home with the empty basket under her arm.

In the morning my brothers and I made a quick check of the presents, then bolted to the place where we had left the treats for Santa. Only the bread crust remained on the plate. The glass was empty. We were ecstatic.

My mother had to remind us about the basket. "Go out and see if the reindeer got their snack," she said.

The basket sat where we'd left it. Not a blade of grass remained. They ate it all!

The proof was as plain as could be. There really *was* a Santa Claus and hungry reindeer. Even in the Philippines without chimneys.

*Steven Goldsberry*

131

# Sumptuous Dessert Buffet

*This gaily decorated snowball cake makes the perfect holiday centerpiece for this luscious array of sumptuous desserts. And what could be more festive than a bountiful bowl of holiday punch?*

## Snowball Cake

1 package (2-layer size) German chocolate, chocolate, *or* pudding cake mix
½ cup raspberry jam, orange marmalade, *or* apricot or cherry preserves
3½ cups frozen non-dairy whipped topping, thawed
1⅓ cups flaked coconut

Preheat oven to 350°. Prepare cake mix as directed on package. Bake in three 8-inch layer pans 30 minutes. Trim ½-inch ring from outer edge of 2 of the layers. Assemble cake, spreading jam between layers. Place trimmed layers on bottom and top, with the full layer in the middle. Frost with whipped topping, rounding edges to resemble the shape of a ball. Sprinkle with coconut. Refrigerate.

**Makes 10 servings.**
Note: See photo for decorating ideas.

**To tint coconut**
Dilute a few drops of food coloring with ½ teaspoon water; add to 1 cup coconut. Toss with fork until evenly tinted.

## Chocolate Cut-Outs

4 squares semi-sweet chocolate, *or* 1 package (4 ounces) German sweet chocolate
1 tablespoon butter *or* margarine

Melt chocolate with butter in saucepan over very low heat, stirring constantly. Pour onto waxed paper-lined baking sheet; spread to about ⅛-inch thickness. Chill until firm, about 15 minutes. Cut with cookie cutters, and immediately lift gently from paper with knife. Chocolate may also be cut into squares, then into triangles. Store on waxed paper in refrigerator or freezer. Use to garnish desserts.

## Golden Almond Torte

1 cup unblanched almonds, toasted
1 package (18.25 oz.) yellow cake mix
1⅓ cups water
3 eggs, separated
⅓ cup butter *or* margarine, softened
1 teaspoon almond extract
Almond Cream Frosting (follows)

Heat oven to 325°. Grease and flour 10-inch springform pan. Reserve ¼ cup almonds, if desired, for garnish. In food processor or blender, process ¾ cup almonds until finely ground. In large mixer bowl, beat cake mix, water, egg yolks, butter, ⅓ cup ground almonds, and almond extract on low speed until blended. Beat 2 minutes on medium speed. Clean beaters. In separate bowl, beat egg whites at high speed until soft peaks form. Gently fold egg whites into cake mix until well blended. Pour into prepared pan. Bake 55 minutes or until wooden pick inserted in center comes out clean. With knife, loosen and remove outer ring of springform pan. Cool completely on wire rack. Prepare Almond Cream Frosting.

To assemble cake; cut cake in half crosswise. Place bottom half of cake on serving plate. Spread with 1½ cups frosting. Top with remaining cake half; spread top and sides with remaining frosting. Sprinkle top and sides with remaining ground almonds. Garnish, if desired, with reserved frosting and almonds.

Makes about 12 servings.

### Almond Cream Frosting

1 envelope unflavored gelatine
¼ cup cold water
¼ cup almond liqueur
2 cups (1 pint) heavy cream
½ cup confectioners' sugar
Almonds, chopped (optional)

Chill large mixing bowl at least 15 minutes. In small saucepan, sprinkle unflavored gelatine on cold water to soften, about 1 minute. Stir over low heat until gelatine is completely dissolved, about 3 minutes. Stir in liqueur. In chilled bowl, beat cream on low speed, gradually adding lukewarm gelatine mixture. Beat on medium speed until thickened, about 5 minutes. Gradually add confectioners' sugar, then beat on high speed until soft peaks form, about 2 minutes. Reserve ⅔ cup frosting, if desired, for garnish.

## Glazed Pecan Puffs

Oil
2½ cups cake flour
5 teaspoons baking powder
1 teaspoon ground nutmeg
1 teaspoon ground cinnamon
½ teaspoon salt
1½ cups milk
1 teaspoon vanilla extract
2 cups pecans, chopped
3 medium apples, grated
Citrus Glaze (follows)

In large bowl, sift together cake flour, baking powder, nutmeg, cinnamon, and salt. Stir in milk and vanilla; add pecans and apples. Heat oil (3 to 4 inches) to 375° in deep fat fryer. Carefully drop by teaspoonfuls into hot oil. Fry, turning once, until golden brown. Drain on paper towels; cool. Pyramid puffs on serving platter and drizzle with Citrus glaze.

Makes about 8 dozen puffs.

### Citrus Glaze

1½ cups confectioners' sugar
2½ tablespoons milk
½ teaspoon grated orange peel
½ teaspoon grated lemon peel

In small bowl, blend all ingredients.

## Trimmer's Punch

1 cup 100% instant tea powder
2 quarts cold water
1 quart cranberry juice cocktail
2 cans (6 ounces each) frozen lemonade concentrate
2 cans (6 ounces each) frozen orange juice concentrate
2 bottles (28 ounces each) seltzer, chilled
Frozen strawberries, thawed and sliced (optional)
Orange slices (optional)

In punch bowl, combine all ingredients except seltzer and fruit; chill. Just before serving, add seltzer, ice and, if desired, fruit slices.

Makes 25 servings.

### Variation

*Adult Trimmer's Punch:* Use 2 bottles (⅘ quart each) rosé wine instead of cold water.

## Hazelnut Cheesecake

1½ cups vanilla wafer crumbs
   (about 25 wafers)
½ cup ground hazelnuts,
   toasted
¼ cup margarine, melted
4 packages (8 ounces each)
   cream cheese, softened
1 cup granulated sugar
4 eggs
1 cup dairy sour cream
3 tablespoons hazelnut liqueur
⅓ cup ground hazelnuts,
   toasted

Heat oven to 325°. Mix wafer crumbs, ½ cup hazelnuts, and margarine thoroughly. Press mixture evenly in bottom of 9-inch springform pan or 13 × 9 inch pan. Bake 10 minutes.

In large mixer bowl, beat cream cheese. Gradually add sugar, beating until fluffy. Beat in eggs, one at a time. Blend in sour cream and liqueur; stir in hazelnuts. Pour over crust. Increase oven temperature to 450°. Bake 10 minutes. Reduce oven temperature to 250°; continue baking 1 hour. Loosen edge of cheesecake from rim of pan with knife. Cool before removing rim of pan. Chill. Garnish with whipped cream and additional hazelnuts, if desired.

**Makes 10 to 12 servings.**

**Variation:** 1 tablespoon vanilla extract and 2 tablespoons milk can be substituted for the hazelnut liqueur.

## Sleighride Spice Cake

1 package spice cake mix
1 can (10¾ ounces) condensed
   tomato soup
½ cup water
2 eggs
1 cup candied fruit, chopped
1 cup walnuts, chopped
   Cream Cheese Frosting
   (follows)

Heat oven as directed on package. Grease and lightly flour two 8 or 9-inch round layer pans. In large bowl, combine cake mix, soup, water, and eggs; beat as directed on package. After mixing, fold in fruit and nuts. Pour into prepared pans. Bake as directed on package, or until wood pick inserted in center comes out clean. Cool on wire racks 10 minutes; remove from pans. Cool completely on racks. Prepare Cream Cheese Frosting. Fill and frost.

**Makes 12 servings.**

### Variations

**Bundt Pan:** Bake in a greased and floured 2-quart bundt pan at 350° for 1 hour or until done. Cool right-side up on wire rack 10 minutes, remove from pan. Cool completely on rack.

**Mincemeat:** Substitute ½ cup prepared mincemeat for fruit. Bake in two 9-inch layers or 13 × 9 inch pan.

**Coconut:** Substitute ½ cup shredded coconut for candied fruit; reduce to ½ cup.

**Date-Nut:** Substitute ½ cup chopped dates for fruit.

**Apricot-Nut:** Substitute 1 cup chopped cooked dried apricots for fruit. Increase walnuts to 1 cup. Bake in 9-inch tube pan at 350° for 1 hour.

### Cream Cheese Frosting

1 package (8 ounces) cream
   cheese, softened
1 package (16 ounces)
   confectioners' sugar
8 tablespoons (1 stick) butter *or*
   margarine
1 teaspoon vanilla extract
½ to 1 cup nuts, chopped
   (optional)

In a large mixer bowl, combine ingredients and beat well.

**Makes 3½ to 4½ cups frosting.**

**Note:** For fluffier frosting, use an electric mixer.

## Mini Herb Cheesecakes

12 pumpernickel crackers
2 packages (8 ounces each)
   cream cheese, softened
2 tablespoons all-purpose flour
1 egg
½ cup dairy sour cream
2 tablespoons chives, chopped
1 tablespoon parsley, chopped
⅛ teaspoon salt
   Dash of pepper
   Red and green pepper strips
   (optional)

Heat oven to 325°. Place crackers, flat side down, on bottom of twelve foil or paper-lined muffin cups. Combine cream cheese and flour, mixing on medium speed until well blended. Add egg and sour cream; mix well. Stir in remaining ingredients. Pour mixture into muffin cups, filling each ¾ full. Bake 25 minutes. Cool before removing from pan. Chill. Garnish with pepper strips, if desired.

**Makes 12 servings.**

## Orange Crown Cake

3 cups all-purpose flour
1 tablespoon baking powder
8 egg whites, room temperature
¼ teaspoon salt
2 cups granulated sugar
1 cup butter *or* margarine, softened
1 teaspoon vanilla extract
1 cup orange juice
1 teaspoon grated orange peel
2 oranges, peeled, sectioned, and drained (optional)
  Pecan halves (optional)
  Candied red cherries (optional)
  Fresh orange sections (optional)
  Orange Frosting (follows)

Heat oven to 350°. Grease and flour three 9-inch layer pans. Stir together flour and baking powder; set aside. In large mixer bowl, beat egg whites with salt until soft peaks form. Gradually beat in ½ cup sugar until peaks are stiff and glossy; set aside. Cream butter, remaining 1½ cups sugar, and vanilla until light. Beat in flour mixture alternately with orange juice until smooth. Stir in orange peel. Gently fold in egg white mixture. Divide batter evenly among prepared pans. Bake 20 to 25 minutes, or until golden brown.

Cool in pans on rack 5 minutes. Remove from pans; cool completely. Prepare Orange Frosting. To assemble cake; spread frosting with fruit and nuts between layers and on sides of cake. Smooth reserved spread on top. Garnish with whole pecan halves, halved red cherries, and orange sections. Cover; store in cool place.

**Makes 10 to 12 servings.**

## Royal Orange Frosting

8 egg yolks
1¼ cups granulated sugar
½ cup butter *or* margarine
2 teaspoons grated orange peel
¾ cup pecans, chopped
¾ cup coconut, shredded
¾ cup candied cherries, chopped
2 Florida oranges, peeled, sectioned, and cut in small pieces

In top of double boiler combine egg yolks, sugar, butter, and orange peel. Stir over simmering water 10 minutes, or until mixture mounds when dropped from a spoon. (Mixture will be slightly transparent.) Remove from heat. Set aside ¼ of the frosting in small bowl; cover. Stir pecans, coconut, cherries, and orange pieces into remaining frosting. Turn into bowl; cover. Chill until of a stiff spreading consistency, several hours, or overnight.

**Fills and frosts a three 9-inch layer cake.**

## Orange Strufoli Wreath

3 cups all-purpose flour, sifted
4 eggs, slightly beaten
1 egg yolk
¼ cup shortening
1 tablespoon granulated sugar
¼ teaspoon salt
1 tablespoon grated orange peel
  Oil for frying
1 cup honey
1 cup orange juice
1 cup granulated sugar
1 tablespoon grated orange peel
¼ cup pine nuts
  Colored sprinkles
1 orange, thinly sliced

In large mixer bowl, add 2½ cups flour; make a "well" in center. Pour eggs and egg yolk, shortening, sugar, salt, and orange peel into "well". Work ingredients together with wooden spoon, then hands, until dough leaves sides of bowl; add remaining ½ cup flour as necessary. On lightly floured board, knead dough until smooth and no longer sticky. Cut off small pieces of dough; roll on floured board into long, narrow ropes. Cut ropes into ½-inch pieces; roll between palms of hands to form tiny balls.

In large, heavy saucepan or deep fryer, heat 2 inches of oil to 375°. Fry one handful of dough balls at a time, about 2 minutes, or until golden brown. Remove with slotted spoon to paper toweling; drain.

In medium-large saucepan over medium heat, heat honey; stir in orange juice, sugar, and orange peel. Bring to a boil; reduce heat and simmer 5 minutes. Add strufoli balls; stir gently with wooden spoon until they are well-coated with syrup. Remove to flat dish with small lip; let cool slightly.

With wet hands, shape strufoli into a wreath. Sprinkle with pine nuts and sprinkles; cool completely. Decorate top and sides with orange slices. Cover with foil; store at room temperature no longer than three days.

**Makes 1 wreath, about 8 servings.**

# Snowflakes

Out of the bosom of the air,
Out of the cloud-folds
    of her garments shaken,
Over the woodland brown and bare,
Over the harvest-fields forsaken,
Silent, and soft, and slow
Descends the snow.

*Henry Wadsworth Longfellow*

# Holiday High Tea

*After the flurry of holiday preparations, share an afternoon of delicate sweets and cordial conversation with a few close friends while the snowflakes swirl outside.*

## Cranberry Fig Bars

- 1 package (12 ounces) fresh cranberries, stems removed
- 1 cup dried figs, snipped
- 6 tablespoons honey
- 1 teaspoon vanilla extract
- 2 cups all-purpose flour
- 2 cups oatmeal
- 1½ cups light brown sugar (packed)
- ½ teaspoon baking soda
- ½ teaspoon ground cinnamon
- ¼ teaspoon salt
- 1 cup butter *or* margarine, melted
  Lemon Glaze (follows)

Heat oven to 350°. In large saucepan, combine cranberries, figs, and honey. Cook, covered, over low heat 15 minutes, or until cranberries pop, stirring frequently. Stir in vanilla. Set filling aside.

In large mixer bowl, stir together flour, oatmeal, sugar, baking soda, cinnamon, and salt. Blend in butter. Pat half oat mixture on bottom of 13 × 9 × 2 inch baking pan. Bake 8 minutes.

Spread filling over baked layer. Sprinkle remaining oat mixture evenly on top, pressing lightly. Bake 20 minutes, or until golden brown. Cool on wire rack. Prepare Lemon Glaze and drizzle over top. Cool, cut into bars, about 2 × 1½ inches.

Makes 28 bars.

### Lemon Glaze

- 1½ cups confectioners' sugar, sifted
- 2 tablespoons lemon juice

In medium bowl, combine ingredients, gradually adding juice until of a spreading consistency.

## Fruit Burst Cookies

1 cup butter *or* margarine
¼ cup granulated sugar
1 teaspoon almond extract
2 cups all-purpose flour
½ teaspoon salt
1 cup nuts, finely chopped
  Fruit Spread

Heat oven to 400°. Cream butter and sugar until light and fluffy. Blend in almond extract. Combine flour and salt. Add to creamed mixture and mix well. Shape level tablespoons of dough into balls; roll in nuts. Place on ungreased cookie sheet; flatten slightly. Press thumb deeply into center of each cookie; spoon small amount of fruit spread into each thumbprint. Bake 10 to 12 minutes, or just until lightly browned.

**Makes 2½ dozen cookies.**

## Cottage Cakes

2¼ cups all-purpose flour
 2 teaspoons baking powder
 ½ teaspoon baking soda
 ¼ teaspoon salt
 1 teaspoon ground cinnamon
 ¼ teaspoon ground nutmeg
 ½ cup butter *or* margarine,
   softened
 ½ cup granulated sugar
 ½ cup light brown sugar
   (packed)
 3 eggs
 1 can (16 ounces) solid pack
   pumpkin
 ¼ cup milk
 2 teaspoon orange zest (page
   152)
 1 cup assorted dried fruits *or*
   raisins, chopped
   Quick Drizzle Frosting
   (follows)

Heat oven to 350°. In medium bowl, combine flour, baking powder, baking soda, salt, cinnamon, and nutmeg; set aside. In large mixer bowl, cream butter and sugars. Add eggs; beat until light and fluffy. Blend in pumpkin, milk, and orange zest. Add dry ingredients; mix well. Stir in chopped fruits. Spoon batter into 20 greased or paper-lined muffin cups, filling ¾ full. Bake 25 to 30 minutes, or until wooden pick inserted in center comes out clean. Immediately remove from pans; cool on wire racks. Drizzle cakes with frosting.

**Makes 20 small cakes.**

### Quick Drizzle Frosting

 1 cup confectioners' sugar,
   sifted
 2 to 3 tablespoons cream *or*
   fresh lemon juice

In small bowl, combine all ingredients.

## Buttermilk Oatmeal Scones

 2 cups all-purpose flour, sifted
 1 cup rolled oats
 1 tablespoon baking powder
 ½ teaspoon baking soda
 ⅛ teaspoon salt
 ⅓ cup granulated sugar
 6 tablespoons cold unsalted
   margarine, cut up
 1 cup buttermilk

Heat oven to 375°. Blend flour, oats, baking powder, baking soda, salt, and sugar. Using a pastry blender or food processor, cut in margarine until mixture is crumbly. Add buttermilk and stir with a fork until a soft dough forms. Turn dough onto floured board; knead 10 to 12 times. Roll out into rectangle ½ inch thick. Cut into 1½-inch circles. Place on lightly buttered baking sheet. Brush tops with small amount of buttermilk and sprinkle with sugar. Bake 18 to 20 minutes, or until golden brown.

**Makes about 30 scones.**

## Pear Mincemeat Oatmeal Bars

¾ cup butter *or* margarine, softened
¾ brown sugar (packed)
1½ cups all-purpose flour
1¼ cups quick rolled oats
½ cup walnuts, chopped
½ teaspoon salt
½ teaspoon baking soda
2 pears, cored and chopped
1 cup prepared mincemeat
1 teaspoon lemon juice
½ teaspoon grated lemon peel

Heat oven to 375°. Cream butter and sugar. Stir in flour, oats, nuts, salt, and baking soda until crumbly. Press ⅔ of crumb mixture into a 13 × 9 × 2 inch pan. Combine pears, mincemeat, lemon juice, and peel; spread over crumb crust. Top with remaining crumb mixture; pat lightly. Bake 25 to 30 minutes or until golden.

**Makes 30 to 35 bars.**

## Pumpkin Scones

2 cups all-purpose flour
½ cup light brown sugar (packed)
2 teaspoons baking powder
½ teaspoon baking soda
¼ teaspoon salt
¾ teaspoon ground cinnamon
¼ teaspoon ground nutmeg
¼ teaspoon ground allspice
¼ cup butter *or* margarine
½ cup golden raisins *or* currants
1 egg, lightly beaten
¾ cup solid pack pumpkin
2 tablespoons buttermilk
1 egg white, beaten

Heat oven to 400°. In large bowl, combine flour, sugar, baking powder, baking soda, salt, cinnamon, nutmeg, and allspice; mix well. Using pastry blender or 2 knives, cut in butter until mixture is crumbly. Stir in raisins; set aside.

In small bowl, combine egg, pumpkin, and buttermilk. Add to dry ingredients; mix well. Turn dough onto lightly floured board; pat dough into circle ¾ inch thick. Using a 2-inch round cutter, cut into 14 scones. Place scones on ungreased cookie sheet. Brush tops with egg white. Bake 10 to 12 minutes, or until wooden pick inserted in center comes out clean. Remove from cookie sheet; cool on wire rack.

**Makes 14 scones.**

## Fruit Spreads

*These spreads can be made with blueberries, blackberries, raspberries, strawberries or any seasonal berry.*

2 cups berries
1½ cups granulated sugar

Wash, drain, and crush fruits. Add sugar. Cook over medium heat until sugar is dissolved, stirring constantly. Increase heat and bring to rapid boil, stirring constantly. Cook 10 minutes, or until jam is thick and a small amount dropped onto a saucer stays in place. Cool completely.

Store covered in the refrigerator no longer than 1 month.

**Makes 2 cups.**

*SAFETY TIP*
When preparing and storing fruit, follow manufacturer's instructions for sealing jar. Label and date.

## Gingerloaf Fingers

2½ cups all-purpose flour
1 teaspoon ground ginger
¾ teaspoon baking soda
¾ teaspoon ground cinnamon
¼ teaspoon ground cloves
1 teaspoon salt
¼ cup light molasses
¾ cup milk
¼ cup margarine
¾ cup granulated sugar
1 egg
Ricotta Spread (follows)

Heat oven to 350°. Grease a 4 × 8 or 5 × 9 inch loaf pan. Sift together dry ingredients. Combine molasses and milk. Cream margarine and sugar until light and fluffy. Add egg and beat well. Add dry ingredients alternately with molasses mixture, beating well after each addition. Pour into loaf pan. Bake 35 to 45 minutes. Cool. Cut into ⅓ inch slices.

**Makes about 30 fingers.**

### Ricotta Spread for Gingerloaf Fingers

1 cup ricotta cheese (part skim)
¼ cup confectioners' sugar
1 teaspoon finely grated orange peel
½ cup dried apricots, finely chopped

Mix all ingredients; blend well. Spread ricotta mixture onto gingerloaf slices to make sandwiches. Slice sandwiches into fingers.

# Elegant Holiday Supper

*For a delightful change of pace, enjoy the sweet sensation of cherries over veal cutlets accompanied by Wild Rice Casserole. Subtle Pistachio Cheesecake completes this simple, elegant supper.*

## Veal Cutlets with Dried Cherry Sauce

> 6 **veal cutlets, about ¼ inch thick**
> **Butter** *or* **margarine**
> **Dried Cherry Sauce (follows)**

On cutting board, with meat mallet, dull edge of French knife, or edge of plate, pound cutlets to ⅛-inch thickness, turning once. In a large skillet over medium-high heat, in hot butter, cook cutlets until lightly browned on both sides. Serve with Dried Cherry Sauce.

**Makes 6 servings.**

### Dried Cherry Sauce

> ½ **cup butter**
> ⅓ **cup dried cherries**
> ¼ **cup heavy cream**
> ½ **cup dry white wine**
> ¼ **teaspoon ground cardamom**

Blend or process butter and cherries until smooth; chill until firm.

Combine cream and wine in saucepan. Bring to boil and reduce to ⅓ cup. Add cardamom. Whisk in cherry-butter by tablespoonfuls. Serve sauce with veal cutlets.

**Makes 1 cup sauce.**

## Wild Rice Casserole with Dried Cherries

⅓ cup butter *or* margarine
1 cup celery, cut diagonally
¾ cup green onion, chopped
⅓ cup fresh parsley, minced
2 cups chicken broth
1½ cups water
¾ cup wild rice
1 teaspoon salt
1 teaspoon fresh marjoram
½ cup long grain white rice
1 cup dried cherries

Heat oven to 350°. Melt butter in a large saucepan. Add celery, onion, and parsley; sauté until tender. Bring chicken broth and 1¼ cups water to boil. Add to sautéed vegetables with wild rice, salt, and marjoram; cover. Bake 1 hour. Stir in white rice and ¼ cup water; cover. Cook 20 minutes. Stir in cherries. Water should be absorbed and rice tender. Fluff casserole with fork.

**Makes 6 servings.**

## Pistachio Cheesecake

3 packages (8 ounces each) cream cheese, softened
1¼ cups granulated sugar
4 eggs, room temperature
2½ teaspoons vanilla extract
1½ teaspoons lemon peel, grated
   **Shortbread Crumb Pastry** (follows)
1 cup dairy sour cream
¾ cup pistachios, chopped

Heat oven to 350°. Prepare Shortbread Crumb Pastry. Beat cream cheese and 1 cup sugar until light and fluffy. Add eggs, one at a time. Add 1½ teaspoons vanilla and lemon peel. Pour cream cheese mixture into Shortbread Crumb Pastry. Bake 30 minutes. Cool on rack 20 minutes. Combine sour cream, ¼ cup sugar, and 1 teaspoon vanilla. Spread over cheesecake. Continue baking 15 minutes. Cool 2 hours on rack. Refrigerate at least 8 hours. Loosen edge of cheesecake with knife before removing side of pan. Press pistachios into side of cheesecake and sprinkle pistachios in center of top.

**Makes 16 servings.**

### Shortbread Crumb Pastry

1½ cups shortbread cookie crumbs
3 tablespoons butter, melted
2 tablespoons pistachios, finely chopped
2 tablespoons granulated sugar

Crumble shortbread cookies. Combine all ingredients. Pat into bottom of 9-inch pan.

How grand and how bright
That wonderful night
When angels to Bethlehem came.
They burst forth like fires
They struck their gold lyres
And mingled their sound with the flame.

*17th Century English Carol*

# Holiday Punches

*"To old friendships and new years." The whole family can enjoy Yuletide toasts with many of our light, fruity punches and teetotaling beverages.*

## Hot Spiced Pineapple Juice

1  can (46 ounces) pineapple
   juice
1  cup apple juice
½  cup brown sugar (packed)
1  teaspoon ground cinnamon
¼  teaspoon ground nutmeg
⅛  teaspoon ground cloves
1  cup light rum *or* 2 teaspoons
   rum extract
   Whole cloves
   Lemon slices

Combine pineapple juice, apple juice, brown sugar and spices in large saucepan or Dutch oven. Simmer 15 minutes. Add rum. Insert cloves into lemon slices; use to garnish mugs.

**Makes 9 servings.**

## Pina Colada Punch

5  cups pineapple juice
1  can (15 ounces) real cream of
   coconut
1  liter (1 quart) lemon-lime
   soda
   Juice of 1 lime
1½ cups light rum (optional)
   Ice cubes
1  lime, thinly sliced
   Mint sprigs

Chill all ingredients. Blend 2 cups pineapple juice with cream of coconut. Combine pureed mixture with remaining pineapple juice, soda, juice of 1 lime, rum, if desired, and ice. Garnish with sliced lime and mint.

**Makes 15 servings.**

## Pineapple Raspberry Punch

5  cups pineapple juice
1  quart raspberry cranberry
   drink
1  pint fresh *or* frozen
   raspberries, thawed
1  lemon, thinly sliced
   Ice

Chill all ingredients. Combine in punch bowl, add ice.

**Makes 9 servings.**

## Cranberry Sangria

6  cups (48 ounces) cranberry
   juice cocktail
3  cups sweet red wine
1  orange, thinly sliced
1  lemon, thinly sliced
   Granulated sugar

In a tall pitcher, mix together cranberry juice, wine, and sliced fruits. Add sugar to taste. Chill several hours to blend flavors. Serve in large wine glasses and garnish with fruit slices.

**Makes 12 servings.**

## Festive Citrus Punch

- 4 oranges
- 24 whole cloves
- 1½ cups cold water
- 1 cup orange juice, fresh squeezed
- ½ cup lemon juice, fresh squeezed
- 2 cans (6 ounces each) unsweetened pineapple juice
- 2 cans (6 ounces each) apple juice
- ⅓ cup granulated sugar
- 1 bottle (28 ounces) lemon-lime soda, chilled
  Cinnamon sticks (optional)

Using a round wooden toothpick or ice pick, puncture the skin of each orange 6 times and insert cloves in holes; chill. In punch bowl, combine water, fruit juices, and sugar; stir to dissolve sugar. Chill. To serve, add chilled oranges and soda. Serve with cinnamon stick stirrers, if desired.

**Makes about 10 servings.**

**Note:** Chilled oranges will keep punch cold while serving.

## Spicy Mulled Milk Punch

- 2 quarts milk
- 12 cloves
- 1 cinnamon stick
- ¼ teaspoon ground nutmeg
- ½ cup granulated sugar
- 2 cups dark rum
- 1 cup fruit brandy (apple, peach, or cherry)
  Softly whipped cream
  Orange zest, for garnish (note)
  Cinnamon sticks, for garnish

Heat milk, cloves, cinnamon stick, nutmeg, and sugar to scalding. Remove from heat; stir in brandy.

Serve warm garnished with whipped cream, orange zest, or cinnamon sticks.

**Makes 15 to 20 servings.**

Note: Orange zest is orange peel with white, pithy part removed, since it is bitter. A kitchen tool called a "zester" is used to peel the slivers, or use a very sharp knife.

## Orange Macaroon

- 2 cups orange juice
- 2 cups crushed ice
- ½ cup real cream of coconut
- ¾ teaspoon almond extract
  Whipped cream (optional)
  Shredded orange peel (optional)

In blender, combine orange juice, ice, coconut cream, and almond extract. Blend until smooth. Serve in chilled glasses. Garnish with whipped cream and orange peel, if desired.

**Makes 4 servings.**

## Merry Berry Holiday Punch

6 cups orange juice
2 cups cranberry juice cocktail
2 packages (10 ounces each) frozen quick-thaw strawberries in syrup
3 cups ginger ale
  Ice
  Orange slices (optional)
  Fresh strawberries (optional)
  Mint (optional)

In a large bowl, combine orange juice, cranberry juice, and strawberries. Add ginger ale and ice just before serving. Float orange slices, strawberries, and mint on top, if desired.

**Makes 18 servings.**

## Tallahassee Tonic

⅔ cup orange juice
½ cup tonic water
  Ice
  Orange or lime wedges (optional)

Pour orange juice and tonic water into a tall, ice-filled glass. Garnish with wedge of fresh orange or lime, if desired.

**Makes 1 serving.**

## Low-Cal Cranberry Sparkler

3 cups low-calorie cranberry juice cocktail, chilled
2 cups low-calorie lemon soda, club soda *or* seltzer, chilled
  Lemon slices

In a tall pitcher, combine cranberry juice and soda or seltzer. Serve in tall glasses over ice. Garnish with lemon slices.

**Makes 6 servings.**

## Sangrita

2 cups orange juice, chilled
2 cups tomato juice, chilled
¼ cup lime juice
3 tablespoons canned green chilies, chopped
2 tablespoons onion, chopped
2 teaspoons Worcestershire sauce
  Orange slices (optional)
  Fresh chili peppers (optional)

In blender, combine orange juice, tomato juice, lime juice, chopped chilies, onion, and Worcestershire. Blend until smooth. Serve in chilled glasses. Garnish with orange slices and fresh chili peppers, if desired.

**Makes 3 to 4 servings.**

## Grapefruit Daiquiri

1 cup grapefruit juice
¾ cup bottled daiquiri mix
1 ripe banana, peeled
1 cup crushed ice

In blender, combine grapefruit juice, daiquiri mix, and banana. Blend until smooth. Add ice and blend a few seconds longer until combined. Serve in daiquiri or cocktail glasses.

**Makes 2 servings.**

## Orange Sour

1 cup orange juice
¾ cup apricot nectar
1 envelope (9/16 ounces) instant whiskey sour drink mixer
½ cup crushed ice
  Orange slices (optional)
  Maraschino cherries (optional)

In blender, combine orange juice, nectar, sour mix, and ice; blend 15 seconds. Pour into tall glasses filled with ice. Garnish with orange slice and maraschino cherry, if desired.

**Makes 2 servings.**

# New Year's Eve Dinner

*Don't have time to prepare an elegant dinner?
Get together with some friends and plan a "progressive" party.
Each person prepares one course, and guests
"progress" from one home to the next. Everyone gets
a chance to be "company" and enjoy the party.*

## Sweet and Savory Triangles

2   tablespoons vegetable oil
1   package (12 ounces) mild sausage meat
1   Granny Smith apple, peeled, cored, and finely diced
1   tablespoon lemon juice
3   cups ice water
½   cup raisins
2   tablespoons apple brandy *or* regular brandy
3   tablespoons unsalted butter
1   medium Spanish onion, finely diced
2   cups fresh *or* frozen cranberries, thawed
2   tablespoons granulated sugar
1   cup walnuts, coarsely chopped
1   teaspoon ground cinnamon
1   teaspoon ground allspice
1½  teaspoons salt
    Freshly ground pepper
1½  cups (about 4 ounces) grated sharp cheddar cheese
¼   cup heavy cream
12  sheets phyllo dough
½   pound unsalted butter, melted
3   cups fresh *or* frozen cranberries, thawed, for garnish (optional)

In a 10-inch skillet, heat oil over medium heat. Add sausage and mash with fork until meat is separated. Cook until no longer pink, about 10 minutes. Drain sausage well; set aside.

### NEW YEAR'S EVE DINNER MENU

**Sweet and Savory Triangles**
**Party Cheese Puff Ring**
**Crown Roast of Pork**
**Mini Mincemeat Tarts**
**Fudgey Fondue**
**Chocolate Lover's Fondue**
**Jeweled Croquebouche**

Place apple and lemon juice in water. Soak raisins in brandy in a small bowl; set aside.

Heat 3 tablespoons butter in large skillet. Add onion. Cook onion until soft. Add 2 cups cranberries and sugar; cook until the cranberries pop and begin to soften, about 10 minutes. Drain apple and add to skillet. Add raisins and brandy. Add walnuts, cinnamon, allspice, salt, and pepper to taste. Cook mixture on medium heat 5 minutes, stirring occasionally. Add sausage and stir to combine. Cook 5 minutes longer. Remove skillet from heat and stir in grated cheese and cream. Cool.

Unwrap phyllo; remove one sheet. Lay it flat on counter, and using a pastry brush, brush with melted butter. Remove another sheet, and put it on top of first and brush again with butter. (Be sure to cover unused phyllo with a damp towel, so that it won't dry out.) Cut phyllo into fifths the short way with a sharp knife. Place ½ tablespoon sausage mixture at the bottom center of the strip. Fold corner across filling, and continue folding as you would a flag until it is completely folded. Place the finished triangles on baking sheet.

To serve, heat oven to 375°. If triangles have been refrigerated, brush with a small amount of melted butter, and bake 10 to 12 minutes on ungreased baking sheet until golden.

If triangles have been frozen, do not defrost. Place directly on ungreased baking sheet. Bake 20 to 25 minutes. Cool 5 minutes before serving. If desired, place remaining 3 cups of cranberries on serving platter. Top with warm phyllo triangles.

**Makes approximately 60 triangles.**

### SPECIAL HINTS

You can make these 24 hours in advance, and keep wrapped in plastic in refrigerator. Or, you can make them weeks in advance, and wrap them tightly in plastic wrap and freeze. Serve on a platter of fresh cranberries for an especially dramatic presentation.

## Party Cheese Puff Ring

1 **envelope onion-mushroom recipe soup mix**
1 **cup milk**
¼ **cup butter or margarine**
1 **cup all-purpose flour**
4 **eggs**
1 **cup shredded Swiss cheese (about 4 ounces)**
2 **tablespoons milk**

Preheat oven to 375°. In medium saucepan, blend onion-mushroom soup mix with 1 cup milk. Add butter and bring just to boiling; stir in flour. Cook over low heat, stirring constantly, until mixture forms a ball. Remove from heat. Beat in eggs, one at a time, beating well after each addition. Stir in ¾ cup cheese.

On greased and lightly floured baking sheet, drop mixture by heaping tablespoons into 12 mounds, slightly touching, to form large circle. Brush with 2 tablespoons milk, then top with remaining cheese. Bake 40 minutes, or until golden. Serve hot.

**Makes 12 appetizers.**

## Crown Roast of Pork

- **8** to 9 pound crown roast of pork
- **1** pound ground pork, cooked and drained
- **5** cups dry bread cubes
- **1** can (14½ ounces) chicken broth
- **½** cup onion, chopped
- **½** cup celery, chopped
- **1** cup walnut halves, toasted
- **1** teaspoon salt
- **¼** teaspoon ground cinnamon
- **¼** teaspoon ground allspice
- **⅛** teaspoon pepper
- **2** cups sliced fresh *or* frozen rhubarb, thawed
- **½** cup granulated sugar

Heat oven to 325°. Place roast, rib-ends-down, in shallow roasting pan. Insert meat thermometer. Roast 1½ hours. Remove from oven. Turn roast, rib-ends-up. Continue roasting 1½ hours, or until meat thermometer registers 155-160°. Remove from oven. Let stand 10 minutes before slicing.

Meanwhile, combine ground pork, bread cubes, broth, onion, celery, walnuts, and seasonings; mix well. In small saucepan, combine rhubarb and sugar; bring to a boil. Pour over bread mixture and mix lightly. Spoon into buttered 2-quart casserole. Cover; bake at 325°, 1½ hours.

**Makes 16 servings.**

## Mini Mincemeat Tarts

- **1** can (20 ounces) crushed pineapple
- **2** cups prepared mincemeat
- **½** cup slivered almonds, toasted
- **1** teaspoon ground allspice
- **3** cups all-purpose flour
- **2** tablespoons granulated sugar
- **¼** teaspoon salt
- **¾** cup butter *or* margarine
- **½** cup water
- **1** egg yolk
- **1** tablespoon cream *or* milk

Heat oven to 375°. Drain pineapple well by pressing out syrup with back of spoon. Mix together pineapple, mincemeat, almonds and allspice, set aside. Combine flour, sugar, and salt. Cut in butter until mixture resembles coarse meal. Add enough water and blend until dough forms a ball. Divide dough into 12 pieces. Roll out on generously floured board to fit 3¾ inch tart tins. Spoon pineapple mixture into each. Top with remaining dough. Flute edges and make slits on top. Combine egg yolk with cream or milk. Brush over tarts. Bake 20 minutes. Reduce heat to 350°; bake 20 minutes.

**Makes 6 tarts.**

## Jeweled Croquebouche

1 cup milk
½ cup butter
1 cup all-purpose flour
4 eggs
1 cup granulated sugar
½ cup cornstarch
4 eggs
1 quart milk, scalded
2 tablespoons candied ginger, chopped
1½ cups granulated sugar
½ cup water
1 tablespoon lemon juice
    Candied fruit and cherries

Heat oven to 425°. In heavy saucepan, bring 1 cup milk and ½ cup butter to boiling. Beat flour in quickly until dough pulls away from sides of pan. Remove from heat. Beat in eggs, one at a time, until smooth. Pipe or drop from teaspoon onto greased baking sheet. (Shapes will be more rounded if piped.) Bake 15 to 20 minutes. Remove, pierce bottom of each *once* with knife.

Combine 1 cup sugar and cornstarch. Beat in 4 eggs, one at a time, until creamy. Whisk hot milk into egg mixture, and return to heat. Stir and cook until thick and bubbly. Add ginger; cool and refrigerate. To fill puffs, insert tip of pastry bag filled with cream filling into pierced bottom of each puff.

Place 1½ cups sugar, water, and lemon juice in heavy saucepan. Heat over medium heat, without stirring, to boiling. Reduce heat; cook until clear and light gold.

Make a circle of puffs on serving platter. Dip the bottom of each of the remaining puffs into the caramel, one at a time. Quickly place each on top of circle, gradually tapering toward the top.

When tree is formed, decorate with fruit and cherries. Drizzle remaining caramel glaze over puffs. Serve the same day prepared.

**Makes 20 servings.**

## Chocolate Lover's Fondue

- 1 **package (12 ounces) semisweet chocolate pieces**
- ¾ **cup light cream *or* half-and-half**
- ½ **cup granulated sugar Fondue Dippers (follows)**

In heavy saucepan over low heat, combine chocolate pieces, cream, and sugar. Stir constantly, until chocolate is melted and mixture is hot. Transfer to fondue pot or chafing dish. Keep warm, and serve with dippers.

**Makes about 2 cups.**

**Variation:** 2 tablespoons kirsch may be added before serving.

**Fondue Dippers**
Prepare a selection of the following: marshmallows, angel food, sponge or pound cake pieces, strawberries, apple slices, banana chunks, pineapple wedges, Mandarin orange segments, cherries, kiwi, pear slices, or other fresh fruit. Brush apple, banana, and pear slices with lemon juice; drain well.

## Fudgey Fondue

- 1 **package (12 ounces) semisweet chocolate pieces**
- ¾ **cup milk**
- 1 **can (14 ounces) sweetened condensed milk (not evaporated) Fondue Dippers (follows)**

In heavy saucepan over low heat, combine chocolate pieces, milk, and condensed milk. Stir constantly, until chocolate is melted and mixture is hot. Transfer to fondue pot or chafing dish. Keep warm, and serve with dippers. If fondue becomes too thick, stir in 1 or 2 tablespoons milk.

**Makes about 3 cups.**

*Tuesday 25th Decr 1804, cloudy*

We fired the swivels at daybreak and each man fired one round. Our officers gave the party a drink of Taffee (rum). We had the best to eat that could be had, and continued firing and frolicking during the whole day. The Savages did not trouble us as we had requested them not to come as it was a great medicine day with us. We enjoyed a Merry Christmas during the day and evening until nine o'clock—all in peace and quietness.

*Ordway*
*Lewis and Clark Expedition*

# Christmastime

## MEMORIES
### 1990

# Christmas Wish List

*For family gift ideas*

What _____ wants for Christmas _____

_____

_____

_____

What _____ wants for Christmas _____

_____

_____

_____

What _____ wants for Christmas _____

_____

_____

_____

What _____ wants for Christmas _____

_____

_____

_____

What _____ wants for Christmas _____

_____

_____

_____

What _____ wants for Christmas _____
_____
_____
_____

What _____ wants for Christmas _____
_____
_____
_____
_____

What _____ wants for Christmas _____
_____
_____
_____
_____

What _____ wants for Christmas _____
_____
_____
_____
_____

What _____ wants for Christmas _____
_____
_____
_____
_____

# Favorite Christmas Memories

# Christmas Cards

Cards Sent _____

_____

_____

_____

_____

_____

_____

_____

_____

_____

_____

_____

Cards Received _____

_____

_____

_____

_____

_____

_____

_____

_____

_____

_____

_____

_____

Cards Sent _____

_____

_____

_____

_____

_____

_____

_____

_____

_____

_____

_____

_____

Cards Received _____

_____

_____

_____

_____

_____

_____

_____

_____

_____

_____

_____

_____

_____

# Seasonal Family Activities

*Special outings and activities during the holidays*

# Holiday Get-Togethers

*For remembering when we got together with family and friends*

*Where We Got Together* _____

*What We Did* _____

_____

_____

_____

_____

_____

_____

_____

_____

_____

_____

_____

_____

_____

*Where We Got Together* _____

*What We Did* _____

_____

_____

_____

_____

_____

_____

_____

_____

_____

170

*Where We Got Together* _____

*What We Did* _____

_____

_____

_____

_____

_____

_____

_____

_____

_____

_____

_____

_____

*Where We Got Together* _____

*What We Did* _____

_____

_____

_____

_____

_____

_____

_____

_____

_____

_____

_____

_____

# Telephone Calls

*Calls Made*

_____
_____
_____
_____
_____
_____
_____
_____
_____
_____
_____
_____
_____
_____
_____
_____
_____
_____
_____
_____
_____
_____
_____
_____
_____
_____
_____

## Calls Received

# Christmas Gifts

*Gifts Given*

_____

_____

_____

_____

_____

_____

_____

_____

_____

_____

_____

_____

_____

_____

_____

_____

_____

_____

_____

_____

_____

_____

_____

_____

_____

## Gifts Received

_____
_____
_____
_____
_____
_____
_____
_____
_____
_____
_____
_____
_____
_____
_____
_____
_____
_____
_____
_____
_____
_____
_____
_____
_____
_____

# How We Spent the Holidays

## Christmas Eve

*Where We Celebrated* _____

*How We Celebrated* _____

_____

_____

_____

_____

_____

_____

_____

_____

_____

_____

_____

_____

_____

_____

_____

_____

_____

_____

_____

_____

_____

_____

# Christmas Day

*Where We Celebrated* _____

*How We Celebrated* _____

_____

_____

_____

_____

_____

_____

_____

_____

_____

_____

_____

_____

_____

_____

_____

_____

_____

_____

_____

_____

_____

_____

# How We Spent the Holidays

### New Year's Eve        New Year's Day

*Where We Celebrated* _____

*How We Celebrated* _____

_____
_____
_____
_____
_____
_____
_____
_____
_____
_____
_____

*Where We Celebrated* _____

*How We Celebrated* _____

_____
_____
_____
_____
_____
_____
_____
_____
_____
_____
_____

# Holiday Favorites

*Stories, Carols, Movies, TV Shows, Poems, Books*

# New Holiday Traditions

*Recipes, Decorations, Activities*

_____
_____
_____
_____
_____
_____
_____
_____
_____
_____
_____
_____
_____
_____
_____
_____
_____
_____
_____
_____
_____
_____
_____
_____
_____
_____
_____
_____
_____

# Special Moments to Treasure

*Photos and other holiday memorabilia*

# Special Moments to Treasure

*Photos and other holiday memorabilia*

# Special Moments to Treasure

*Photos and other holiday memorabilia*

# HOLIDAY DATEBOOK

## 1990

**NOVEMBER**

**Thursday**
**22**
■ **Thanksgiving Day**
(United States)

**Friday**
**23**

**Saturday**
**24**

**Sunday**
**25**

**Monday**
**26**

**Tuesday**
**27**

**Wednesday**
**28**

**Thursday**
**29**

Friday
30

DECEMBER

Saturday
1

Sunday
2

Monday
3

Tuesday
4

Wednesday
5

Thursday
6

Friday
7

Saturday
8

Sunday
9

Monday
10

| |
|---|
| Tuesday<br>**11** |
| Wednesday<br>**12** |
| Thursday<br>**13** |
| Friday<br>**14** |
| Saturday<br>**15** |
| Sunday<br>**16** |
| Monday<br>**17** |
| Tuesday<br>**18** |
| Wednesday<br>**19** |
| Thursday<br>**20** |
| Friday<br>**21** |

| Saturday **22** | |
|---|---|
| Sunday **23** | |
| Monday **24** | ■ Christmas Eve |
| Tuesday **25** | ■ Christmas Day |
| Wednesday **26** | ■ Boxing Day (Canada) |
| Thursday **27** | |
| Friday **28** | |
| Saturday **29** | |
| Sunday **30** | |
| Monday **31** | |
| | JANUARY |
| Tuesday **1** | ■ New Year's Day |

# ACKNOWLEDGMENTS

The publisher would like to thank those who generously granted permission for use of the following:

**TEXT**

"Letter from Santa Claus" from MY FATHER, MARK TWAIN by Clara Clemens. Copyright 1931 by Clara Clemens Gabrilowitsch. Copyright renewed 1958 by Clara Clemens Samossoud. Reprinted by permission of Harper & Row, Publishers, Inc.

"Candles in the Dark" by Thelma Chang. Reprinted with permission from ALOHA, THE MAGAZINE OF HAWAI'I AND THE PACIFIC.

"The Tree That Didn't Get Trimmed" from ESSAYS by Christopher Morley. Copyright 1931 by Christopher Morley, renewed © 1959 by Helen F. Morley. Reprinted by permission of Harper & Row, Publishers, Inc.

"Bittersweet Christmas" by Madeline Weatherford. Reprinted with permission from THE NEW GUIDEPOSTS CHRISTMAS TREASURY. Copyright © 1988 by Guideposts Associates, Inc., Carmel, NY 10512.

"The Tree" excerpt from CHRISTMAS GIFT! by Ferrol Sams (Longstreet Press). Reprinted by permission of Jed Mattes Inc., New York. All rights reserved. Copyright © 1989 by Ferrol Sams. All rights reserved.

"The Computer's First Christmas Card" from POEMS OF THIRTY YEARS by Edwin Morgan. Copyright © 1982 by Edwin Morgan. Reprinted with permission of Carcanet Press Limited.

"The Man Who Missed Christmas" by J. Edgar Park. Reprinted with permission from THE NEW GUIDEPOSTS CHRISTMAS TREASURY. Copyright © 1988 by Guideposts Associates, Inc., Carmel, NY 10512.

"The Gift of Sharing" by Doris Crandall. Reprinted with permission from THE NEW GUIDEPOSTS CHRISTMAS TREASURY. Copyright © 1988 by Guideposts Associates, Inc., Carmel, NY 10512.

"Sincerely..." by Sue Monk Kidd. Reprinted with permission from THE NEW GUIDEPOSTS CHRISTMAS TREASURY. Copyright © 1988 by Guideposts Associates, Inc., Carmel, NY 10512.

"Even Without Chimneys" (retitled: "The Philippines Without Chimneys") by Steven Goldsberry. Reprinted with permission from ALOHA, THE MAGAZINE OF HAWAI'I AND THE PACIFIC.

**ILLUSTRATIONS**

Title Page, p. 161. Copyright © 1990 by Jeanette Martone.

pp.14-15 The Corning Musuem of Glass, Corning, NY.

pp.16-17 Illustrations from THE CHRIST CHILD by Maud and Miska Petersham, copyright 1931 by Maud and Miska Petersham. Used by permission of Doubleday, a division of Bantam, Doubleday, Dell Publishing Group, Inc.

pp. 24-25, 98-99 paper courtesy of Contempo.®

pp. 34-35 Copyright © 1989 by Michael S. Furuya. Reprinted with permission from ALOHA, THE MAGAZINE OF HAWAI'I AND THE PACIFIC.

p. 54 Copyright © 1990 by Kevin Hand.

pp. 84-85 Copyright © 1990 by Jeanette Martone.

p. 94 Copyright © 1990 by Michael S. Furuya.

p. 100 Copyright © 1990 by Kevin Hand.

p. 112 Copyright © 1990 by Michael S. Furuya.

p. 130 Copyright © 1989 by Kevin Hand. Reprinted with permission from ALOHA, THE MAGAZINE OF HAWAI'I AND THE PACIFIC.

**PHOTOGRAPHS**

pp. 3, 12-13, 22-23, 24-25, 26, 64-65, 93, 98-99, 118-119, 140-141, 148-149, 160 Courtesy of Eastman Kodak Company.

pp. 6-7 Courtesy of NASA.

pp. 8-9 "Spirit of Seattle" Courtesy, Seattle Department of Parks and Recreation. "Salvation Army" The Salvation Army, Greater New York Division. "Decorated Saguaro Cactus" Bob Rink, photographer. Courtesy of City of Phoenix. "Luminarias" Ron Behrmann, photographer. Courtesy of Albuquerque Convention and Visitors Bureau. " Parade of Lights" Courtesy of The Denver Partnership, Inc.

p. 10 Courtesy of National Park Service, National Capital Region.

p. 11 The Western Reserve Historical Society, Cleveland, Ohio.

p. 36 Robert H. Epstein, photographer. Copyright © 1983 by CBS Publications, The Consumer Publishing Division of CBS, Inc. Used by permission of Woman's Day ® magazine.

p. 51 Robert H. Epstein, photographer. Copyright © 1985 by CBS Magazines, a Division of CBS Inc. Used by permission of Woman's Day ® magazine.

p. 70 Thomas Famighetti, photographer. Used by permission of Thomas Famighetti.

p. 87 Schecter Lee, photographer. Used by permission of Schecter Lee.

pp. 88-89 Robert H. Epstein, photographer. Copyright © 1986 by CBS Magazines, a Division of CBS, Inc. Used by permission of Woman's Day® magazine.

**CRAFTS**

pp. 28-31 Angel Candle Holder; pp. 56-61 Nativity Tree Skirt; pp. 72-73 Christmas Tree Sweater; pp. 82-83 Partridge in a Pear Tree from AN OLD-FASHIONED CHRISTMAS by Diana Mansour copyright © Marshall Cavendish Limited 1988, published by Sedgewood® Press, a division of Meredith Corporation.

pp. 32-33 Cinnamon Stick Wreath; pp. 43-46 Patchwork Ornaments; pp. 66-68 Red Warm-Up Set; pp. 68-69 Blue Warm-Up Set from CHRISTMAS AT HOME FROM MCCALL'S NEEDLEWORK & CRAFTS copyright © 1985 by McCall's Needlework & Crafts Magazines, Inc., published by Sedgewood® Press, a division of Meredith Corporation.

pp. 36-39 Folk Art Ornaments from WOMAN'S DAY DOUGHCRAFTS by Lorraine Bodger copyright © 1983 by CBS Publications, The Consumer Publishing Division of CBS, Inc., published by Sedgewood® Press, a division of Meredith Corporation.

pp. 40-42, Bright and Pretty Dough Trims; pp. 78-81 Especially for Babies from CHRISTMAS CRAFTS FROM MCCALL'S NEEDLEWORK & CRAFTS copyright © 1984 by McCall's Needlework & Crafts Magazines, Inc., published by Sedgewood® Press, a division of Meredith Corporation.

pp. 50-53 Small Heart Wreaths from CHRISTMAS TREE ORNAMENTS by Lorraine Bodger copyright © 1985 by CBS Magazines, a division of CBS Inc., published by Sedgewood® Press, a division of Meredith Corporation.

pp. 69-71 Pretty Gauntlet Mittens from CARRY-ALONG CROCHET by Leslie Linsley copyright © 1985 by Leslie Linsley Enterprises, published by Sedgewood® Press, a division of Meredith Corporation.

pp. 74-76 Train Vest from KNIT ONE FOR THE KIDS copyright © Marshall Cavendish Limited 1986, published by Sedgewood® Press, a division of Meredith Corporation.

pp. 86-87 Christmas Hearts Place Mats and Napkin Rings; Reindeer Pot Holder and Apron Set from CELEBRATIONS IN CROSS-STITCH by Lisbeth Perrone copyright © 1988 by Dina von Zweck, published by Sedgewood® Press, a division of Meredith Corporation.

pp. 88-92 Gumdrop Express from SWEET DREAMS OF GINGERBREAD by Jann Johnson copyright © 1986 by CBS Magazines, a division of CBS, Inc., published by Sedgewood® Press, a division of Meredith Corporation.

## RECIPES

pp. 102-104 Photo and recipes: Nut and Pumpkin Pound Cake; Holiday Fruitcakes; Chocolate Pumpkin Truffles; Holiday Almond Treats; Autumn Jam. Courtesy of Libby's Pumpkin, a division of Carnation Company.

pp. 104-105 Photo and recipes: Golden Crown Honey Pound Cake; Honey Roasted Bridge Mix; Brandied Maraschino Cherries. Courtesy of the National Honey Board and the National Cherry Foundation.

pp. 105-107 Photo and recipes: Glazed Colonial Cranberry Breads; Cranberry-Apricot Tea Cakes; Fruitful Cranberry Conserve. Courtesy of Ocean Spray Cranberries, Inc.

p. 106 Recipe: Grandma's Favorite Molasses Fruitcake. Courtesy Sunkist Growers, Inc.

p. 107 Photo and recipe: Orange Cranberry Cake. Courtesy Dole®.

pp. 108-109 Photo and recipe: Bouillabaisse. Courtesy of National Fish and Seafood Promotional Council.

pp. 109-110 Photos and recipes: Spinach Cheese Loaf; Seasoned Bread Ring. Courtesy of Fleischmann's Yeast, a division of Specialty Brands Inc.

p. 111 Photo and recipe: Rice Pudding with Raspberry Sauce and Creme Anglaise. Courtesy of Rice Council for Market Development.

pp. 114-116 Photo and recipes: Chocolate Chip Fruit and Nut Bars; Peanut Butter Glazed Chocolate Bars; Chocolate Cherry Cookies; Butter-Nut Chocolate Topped Cookies. Courtesy of Hershey Foods Corporation.

pp. 116-117 Photo and recipes: Mocha-Frosted Drops; Hazelnut Chip Sandies. Courtesy of Sun-Diamond Growers of California.

pp. 120-121 Photo and recipes: Christmas Beef Standing Rib Roast; Yorkshire Popovers. Provided by California Beef Council.

p. 122 Photo and recipe: Fig Amaretto Cake. Courtesy of California Fig Advisory Board.

p. 123 Photo and recipe: Elegant Berry Trifle. Courtesy of J. M. Smucker Company.

p. 124-126 Photo and recipes: Tangerine Stuffing; Spiced Oranges; Orange Carrot Puff; Orange Holiday Cake. Provided by Florida Department of Citrus.

p. 127 Photo and recipe: Christmas Tree Cheese Spread. Courtesy of Thomas J. Lipton, Inc.

pp. 128-129 Photo and recipes: Easy Chicken Peanut Dip; Tomato Ginger Punch; Spicy Vegetable Punch; Crunchy Chicken Bits. Courtesy of Campbell Soup Company.

pp. 132-133 Photo and recipes: Snowball Cake; Chocolate Cut-Outs. Compliments of General Foods USA.

pp. 134-135 Photo and recipes: Golden Almond Torte; Glazed Pecan Puffs; Trimmer's Punch. Courtesy of Thomas J. Lipton, Inc.

pp. 136-137 Photo and recipes: Hazelnut Cheesecake; Mini Herb Cheesecakes. Courtesy of Kraft, Inc.

p. 136 Recipe: Sleighride Spice Cake. Courtesy of Campbell Soup Company.

p. 136 Recipe: Cream Cheese Frosting. Courtesy Mary K. Weadock.

pp. 138-139 Photo and recipes: Orange Crown Cake; Orange Strufoli Wreath. Provided by Florida Department of Citrus.

p. 142 Photo and recipe: Cranberry Fig Bars. Courtesy of California Fig Advisory Board.

p. 143 Photo and recipe: Fruit Burst Cookies. Courtesy of J. M. Smucker Company.

p. 143 Recipe: Cottage Cakes. Courtesy of Libby's Pumpkin, a division of Carnation Company.

p. 143 Recipe: Buttermilk Oatmeal Scones. Courtesy of The Sugar Association, Inc.

pp. 144-145 Photo and recipe: Pear Mincemeat Oatmeal Bars. Courtesy of Oregon-Washington-California Pear Bureau.

p. 145 Recipe: Pumpkin Scones. Courtesy of Libby's Pumpkin, a division of Carnation Company.

p. 145 Recipes: Fruit Spreads; Gingerloaf Fingers. Courtesy of The Sugar Association, Inc.

pp 146-147 Photo and recipes: Veal Cutlets with Dried Cherry Sauce; Wild Rice Casserole with Dried Cherries. Courtesy of Cherry Central Cooperative Inc., Traverse City, Michigan (616-946-1860).

p. 147 Photo and recipe: Pistachio Cheesecake. Courtesy of California Pistachio Commission.

pp. 150-151 Photos and recipes: Hot Spiced Pineapple Juice; Pina Colada Punch; Pineapple Raspberry Punch. Courtesy of Dole®.

p. 150 Recipe: Cranberry Sangria. Courtesy of Ocean Spray Cranberries, Inc.

p. 152 Photo and recipe: Spicy Mulled Milk Punch. Courtesy of California Milk Advisory Board.

p. 152 Recipe: Festive Citrus Punch. Courtesy of Sunkist Growers, Inc.

p. 153 Recipe: Low-Cal Cranberry Sparkler. Courtesy of Ocean Spray Cranberries, Inc.

pp. 152-153 Recipes: Orange Macaroon; Merry Berry Holiday Punch; Orange Sour; Sangrita; Tallahassee Tonic; Grapefruit Daiquiri. Provided by Florida Department of Citrus.

p. 154 Photo and recipe: Sweet and Savory Triangles. Courtesy of Ocean Spray Cranberries, Inc.

p. 155 Photo and recipe: Party Cheese Puff Ring. Courtesy of Thomas J. Lipton, Inc.

pp. 156-157 Photo and recipe: Crown Roast of Pork. Courtesy National Pork Producers Council.

p. 157 Photo and recipe: Mini Mincemeat Tarts. Courtesy of Dole®.

p. 158 Photo and recipe: Jeweled Croquebouche. Courtesy of California Milk Advisory Board.

p. 159 Photo and recipe: Chocolate Lover's Fondue; Fudgey Fondue. Courtesy of Hershey Foods Corporation.

Special thanks to the following:

Jane Bennett and Ron Behrmann, Albuquerque Visitors and Convention Bureau. Meredithe Samselsky, Chamber of Commerce, Cape May, NJ. Cheryl Chee Tsutsumi, Aloha, The Magazine of Hawai'i and the Pacific. Katherine Kohl, The Lake View Cemetery Association, Cleveland, OH. Virginia Wright, The Corning Museum of Glass, Corning, NY. The Denver Partnership, Inc., Denver, CO. Ed Fortuna, Image Center, Eastman Kodak Company, Rochester, NY. George Tselos, Edison National Historic Site, West Orange, NJ. Robert H. Van Sickler and Frank Laguisa, General Electric Company, Cleveland, OH. Ruth Shoemaker, Hall of History Foundation, General Electric Company, Schenectady, NY. Bob Rink, the City of Phoenix, AZ. Helen F. Davis, The Salvation Army of Greater New York, New York, NY. Andy Reynolds, Seattle Department of Parks and Recreation, Seattle, WA.

# INDEX